EXOTIC CURRIES

EXOTIC CURRIES

Saroj Hadley

IVY LEAF

CONTENTS

NOTES

All recipes serve four unless otherwise stated.
All spoon measurements are level.
All eggs are sizes 3, 4, 5 unless otherwise stated.
Preparation times given are an average calculated during recipe testing.
Metric and imperial measurements have been calculated separately.
Use one set of measurements only as they are not interchangeable.
Cooking times may vary slightly depending on the individual oven.
Dishes should be placed in the centre of the oven unless otherwise specified.
Always preheat the oven or grill to the specified temperature.

ACKNOWLEDGEMENTS

We should like to thank the following who were concerned in the preparation of the book:
Photographer Chris Knaggs with stylists Alison Williams and Andrea Lambton
Food prepared for photography by Jackie Burrow, Margot Mason and Hilary Foster
Step-by-step illustrations by Tony Randell

First published in 1983 by
Octopus Books Limited
part of Reed International Books

This edition published in 1992 by
Ivy Leaf
Michelin House
81 Fulham Road
London SW3 6RB

INTRODUCTION

The recipes in this book reflect different styles of curries from regions of India and are influenced by Asian communities living in Uganda and in Britain. All the ingredients used are readily obtainable in large supermarkets or specialist Asian shops.

Curries are always geared to flexibility and it is not essential to stick rigidly to a recipe. The amounts of spices and seasonings are given as a guide.

It is advantageous to make a curry at least a few hours in advance, or even better, the day before, as the spices have time to develop their flavour.

Foods suitable for currying
Fish
The use of different cuts such as fillets, cutlets and steaks gives a wide scope to create interesting dry and moist fish curries. The use of shellfish in curries undoubtedly enhances their exotic flavour.

Meat
Traditionally meat curries contain pieces of meat cut into bite-sized pieces and cooked in a curry sauce. However, all kinds of cuts of meat are suitable for curry making, for example, chops or joints.

Poultry
Chicken has always been the most popular of meats used in curry making, as there are no taboos on its use on any religious grounds.

Skinning a chicken for Indian cooking (page 46) is essential as the bare flesh allows the flavours of the spices to penetrate.

Pulses
Pulses play an important role in traditional curry making. Canned pulses are used in the recipes but can be substituted with dried.

Dried pulses should be picked over before soaking to remove any grit or stones. They should then be soaked overnight and rinsed in several changes of water. Pre-soaking usually cuts cooking time by half.

As salt tends to harden pulses, it should not be added until the end of cooking.

When using dried kidney beans, soak the beans and ensure they are then boiled for 10 minutes and simmered until completely cooked.

Vegetables
Vegetable curries are as popular as meat curries. They add extra interest to an Indian meal whether cooked dry or with a little sauce.

Frozen vegetables such as peas and spinach are used in some recipes because they are always available. Fresh vegetables may be used if preferred.

Preparing the food
When preparing curries, it is worth bearing these points in mind:

In some recipes, the onions are finely chopped or minced. This is recommended as the flavour will be distinctly improved. Similarly, garlic can be creamed (page 44) to improve the flavour of the dish.

Frying spices and seeds in oil or butter before using in a recipe brings out the flavour of the spices. They should be fried over a low heat, stirring continuously to prevent burning.

Some recipes require ingredients to be fried in several separate stages, even if only for a few seconds. These stages are important and will significantly improve the flavour of the curry.

Special spices and seasonings
Asafoetida (Hing)
This is used widely in Gujarat and Southern India for flavouring vegetable curries and fish. It is a strong smelling gum sold in lumps or ground.

Cardamoms (Elchi)
The pod may be used whole or the black seeds may be separated from the pod when crushed. Crushing the pod imparts a distinctly pleasant flavour.

Chilli (Marcha)
Fresh green or red chillis are extremely hot and should be used sparingly, finely chopped and well mixed into the food (page 69). Wash your hands immediately after preparing as the juice can cause a burning sensation. Powdered chilli is available in most supermarkets.

Cinnamon (Tej)
The stripped bark of a Cassia tree curls into 'quills' as it dries. In Indian cookery the quills are used broken into smaller pieces. Ground cinnamon can be used as a convenient substitute.

Cloves (Luving)
Cloves are aromatic and are used whole in rice dishes and meat curries. To get the full flavour of cloves, they should be fried in hot oil or ghee first.

Coriander (Dhania or Dhanna)
Coriander seeds are used either whole or ground, while fresh coriander is used for flavouring curries and for garnishing.

Cumin (Jeeroo)
The seeds resemble caraway seeds but have a different flavour. Used whole to flavour vegetable curries, ground cumin is used in most meat curries.

Fennel
Not to be confused with aniseed. Fennel seeds have a subtle, slightly bitter aniseed flavour. They are pale yellow to green in colour and can be used crushed.

Fenugreek (Methi)
The golden yellow seeds are used whole in vegetable curries. They are bitter in taste. Powdered seeds are a basic ingredient of curry powder.

Garam Masala
A mixture of selected herbs and spices, garam masala powder is the main seasoning for meat curries. It is available in most supermarkets.

Ginger (Adda)
Fresh root ginger is used in making rice dishes, meat curries and sweet dishes. The root is peeled and used sliced or chopped.

Mustard (Rai)
Black mustard seeds are used whole to flavour vegetable and pulse curries. The seeds are sold in Asian food stores and many health food shops.

Nutmeg
Ground nutmeg imparts a warming flavour to curry sauces.

Turmeric
Turmeric powder is mainly used to colour savoury food, where added colour is necessary in the presentation of the finished dish.

Special ingredients
Coconut cream is available in large supermarkets and Asian food shops. It is the first concentrated extract of fresh coconut.

Canned tomatoes: where recipes use canned tomatoes, the juice is always included.

Fats: Butter, margarine and oil have been used in the recipes. These may be substituted with ghee (clarified butter) which is widely used in Indian cooking. Ghee is available from some specialist Indian food shops but can easily be made at home. The best ghee is made from unsalted butter and will keep for 3–4 months in a cool place.

To make about 350 g (12 oz) ghee, melt 450 g (1 lb) unsalted butter in a saucepan. Slowly simmer the melted butter for 15–20 minutes until it becomes clear and a whitish residue settles at the bottom. Remove from the heat and spoon off any foam. Cool, then strain the clear oil from the top into a container and refrigerate.

Freezing
1. Most curries are suitable for freezing except those which contain potatoes, where the texture of the dish is likely to deteriorate during storage.

2. To freeze curries or convenient quantities of curry sauce, fill a suitably sized plastic freezer container with the curry or sauce leaving at least 1 cm (½ inch) head space. Cool, tightly seal, then label. Place the container in a freezer bag and seal.

The additional freezer bag prevents the flavours penetrating other foods in the freezer.

3. Spices develop their flavours during freezing therefore curries are best used within 1 month.

4. To reheat: thaw the curry or sauce. Place in a saucepan and bring to the boil. Boil for 3 minutes, then simmer until thoroughly heated through.

To serve curries
Garnishes: As a rule, curries are served with a simple garnish, such as coriander, either as a sprig or chopped up. For 4 people, serve a selection of 2 meat or fish and 2 vegetable curries, accompanied by chapatis and/or rice. Chapatis can be ordered from Indian restaurants. Suggestions for particular accompanying dishes are given with some of the recipes.

Rice
Basmati rice should be used to achieve the authentic flavour of a true Indian meal. It is easily obtainable in supermarkets and all Asian shops. The rice should be picked over, washed and then simmered over a low heat using 2 parts or less of water to 1 part of rice. Basmati rice is best cooked without salt as this impairs the natural flavour.

Drinks
There are no rules about drinking wines and beers with an Indian meal.

Generally, wine is unsuitable for hot or medium hot curries as it causes a slight burning sensation in the mouth. Medium sweet or rosé wines can be recommended. Beer and lager are also excellent drinks to serve with curries.

Lassi is a cool yogurt-based drink ideal for serving with spicy food. To serve 4, beat together 300 ml (½ pint) plain yogurt, 1.2 litres (2 pints) water, 50 g (2 oz) caster sugar and a pinch of salt. Serve with ice cubes.

FISH

BASIC CURRY SAUCE

100 g (4 oz) butter
1 large onion, peeled and finely chopped
2 cloves garlic, peeled and creamed
50 g (2 oz) piece of fresh ginger, peeled and chopped
2 tablespoons ground coriander
1 teaspoon garam masala powder
1 teaspoon chilli powder
1 teaspoon ground cardamom
1 × 400 g (14 oz) can tomatoes, chopped with the juice
1 × 75 g (3 oz) can tomato purée
2 teaspoons sugar
150 ml (¼ pint) water
salt

Preparation time: 15–20 minutes
Cooking time: 30 minutes

1. Heat the butter in a saucepan over a medium heat and fry the onion until golden brown.
2. Add the garlic and ginger and fry for a few seconds. Add the spices and fry for 2 minutes, stirring continuously. Stir in the tomatoes and tomato purée and fry for a further 2 minutes.
3. Add the sugar, water and salt and stir well. Partly cover, and cook the sauce over a gentle heat for about 15 minutes, or until the sauce becomes thick and most of the liquid has evaporated.

FISH IN COCONUT AND LEMON

1 small onion, peeled and minced
25 g (1 oz) desiccated coconut
25 g (1 oz) coconut cream, grated
salt
2 tablespoons oil
1 teaspoon turmeric
4 medium plaice fillets, washed and dried
25 g (1 oz) butter
1 tablespoon ground coriander
1 teaspoon chilli powder
1 teaspoon garlic powder
1 teaspoon garam masala powder
4 tablespoons mayonnaise
4 tablespoons double cream
grated rind and juice of 1 lemon
1 lemon, sliced, to garnish

MAKAI MATCHI
(FISH IN CREAMED CORN)

4 coley fillets, about 175 g (6 oz) each
50 g (2 oz) butter
1 medium onion, peeled and minced
2 cloves garlic, peeled and creamed
2 teaspoons cumin seeds, crushed
1 × 300 g (11 oz) can creamed sweetcorn or 1 × 300 g (11 oz) can sweetcorn kernels, drained and liquidized to a smooth cream
1 tablespoon chopped fresh coriander leaves
salt
2 sprigs fresh coriander leaves, to garnish

Preparation time: 30 minutes
Cooking time: 35-40 minutes
Oven: 180°C, 350°F, Gas Mark 4

1. Wash and pat the fish dry using paper towels, then place in a shallow ovenproof dish.
2. Melt the butter in a saucepan over a gentle heat and fry the onion, garlic and cumin for 5–7 minutes, stirring occasionally.
3. Add the creamed corn, fresh coriander and salt. Stir thoroughly, then pour the mixture over the fish. Cover and cook in a preheated oven for 25–30 minutes. Garnish with the coriander sprigs. Serve with a side salad, rice and chapatis.

Preparation time: 30 minutes
Cooking time: 25 minutes
Oven: 180°C, 350°F, Gas Mark 4

1. In a bowl mix together the onion, coconut, coconut cream, salt, oil and turmeric, then rub the mixture over both sides of the fish.
2. Place the fish on a greased baking sheet and bake in a preheated oven for 20 minutes.
3. To make the sauce, melt the butter in a frying pan over a low heat and add the spices. Fry gently for 2–3 minutes, stirring constantly to avoid burning.
4. Add the remaining ingredients, stir well and heat thoroughly without boiling. Place fish on a serving dish and pour the sauce over. Garnish with lemon.

FROM THE BOTTOM: Makai matchi: Fish in coconut and lemon

COPRA MATCHI (FISH IN COCONUT)

4 cod fillets, about 175 g (6 oz) each
2 medium onions, peeled and finely minced
4 tablespoons oil
1 teaspoon chilli powder
25 g (1 oz) desiccated coconut
25 g (1 oz) ground cumin
good pinch of turmeric
salt
50 g (2 oz) coconut cream, grated
1 lemon, cut into quarters, to garnish

Preparation time: 30 minutes
Cooking time: 20–25 minutes

The accent in this mild curry is on coconut which is used in two different forms: desiccated coconut and grated coconut cream.

1. Wash and pat the fish dry using paper towels.
2. In a bowl mix together all the ingredients except the grated coconut cream, then spread the mixture in the base of a frying pan.
3. Place the fish on the bed of mixture and fry each side gently for 7–10 minutes.
4. Transfer the cooked fish and spiced mixture to a heated serving dish, sprinkle with the grated coconut cream and place under a preheated grill for 2–3 minutes to brown.
5. Garnish with the lemon quarters and serve immediately as a starter.

It may come as a surprise to learn that fish is widely used in Indian cooking. There are some 2000 different varieties to choose from, and a correspondingly wide range of cooking methods. Fish can be found roasted, fried, grilled, baked, poached and steamed, the spices used to create the finished dish varying widely from one state to another. A more elaborate method of serving fish curry is to first cook the fish in a spiced mixture and then to serve it with a spicy, creamy sauce (see page 8).

MACKEREL ANGOOR

50 g (2 oz) butter
2 whole medium or 4 whole small mackerel, gutted, cleaned and heads removed
1 medium onion, peeled and finely chopped
1 clove garlic, peeled and creamed
450 g (1 lb) green grapes, halved and seeds removed
1 teaspoon ground nutmeg
1 teaspoon chilli powder
1 teaspoon ground cumin
salt

Preparation time: 20 minutes
Cooking time: 30 minutes
Oven: 180°C, 350°F, Gas Mark 4

1. Melt the butter in a frying pan and quickly fry the fish for 1 minute on each side. Using a slotted fish slice, drain and transfer the fish to a shallow ovenproof dish.
2. Fry the onion and garlic for 2–3 minutes in the remaining juices. Reserve 20 grape halves for garnish and chop half the remaining grapes. Add the nutmeg, chilli, cumin, chopped grapes, grape halves and salt and fry quickly for a further 2–3 minutes.
3. Pour the mixture evenly over the fish. Cover and cook in a preheated oven for 25–30 minutes.
4. Garnish with the reserved halves of the fruit and serve with a green salad, Father's safari potatoes (page 73), pickles and chutneys.

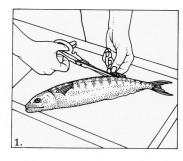
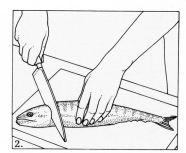
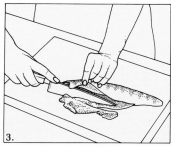

1. Cut off the fins with scissors and trim tail.

2. Cut off the head just below the gills.

3. Slit along the belly and remove innards.

FROM THE LEFT: Mackerel angoor; Copra matchi

MAKHAN MATCHI
(FISH IN CREAMY CURRY SAUCE)

4 medium plaice fillets
½ quantity Basic curry sauce (page 8)
150 ml (¼ pint) double cream
grated rind and juice of 1 lemon
sprigs fresh coriander leaves, to garnish

Preparation time: 10 minutes
Cooking time: 25–30 minutes
Oven: 180°C, 350°F, Gas Mark 4

1. Wash and pat the fish dry using paper towels.
Place, slightly overlapping, in a large shallow ovenproof dish.
2. Combine the curry sauce, double cream, lemon
rind and juice and mix well. Pour the sauce evenly
over the fish. Cover and cook in a preheated oven for
25–30 minutes.
3. Serve garnished with coriander sprigs.

FISH TANDOORI

4 halibut steaks, about 175 g (6 oz) each
50 ml (2 fl oz) plain unsweetened yogurt
2 tablespoons oil
2 tablespoons paprika
1 tablespoon ground cumin
1 teaspoon ground fennel seeds
1 teaspoon chilli powder
salt
1 small lettuce, cleaned and shredded, to serve
1 fennel bulb, sliced, to garnish

Preparation time: 30 minutes, plus marinating
Cooking time: 20–25 minutes
Oven: 180°C, 350°F, Gas Mark 4

1. Wash and pat the fish dry using paper towels.
2. In a large bowl combine all the remaining ingredients and mix well. Place the fish in the bowl
and rub well with the tandoori mixture. Cover and
leave to marinate for 4–5 hours.
3. Transfer the marinated fish to a shallow baking
dish (preferably ovenproof glass) and bake uncovered in a preheated oven for 20–25 minutes.
4. Arrange the lettuce on a warmed serving dish.
Using a slotted fish slice, lift the fish on to the lettuce
and spoon the juices over the fish. Serve immediately, garnished with the fennel.

FROM THE LEFT: Makhan matchi: Fish tandoori

KARACHALA CURRY (CRAB CURRY)

100 g (4 oz) butter
1 medium onion, peeled and finely chopped
1 clove garlic, peeled and creamed
1 tablespoon chopped fresh coriander leaves
1 teaspoon ground nutmeg
1 teaspoon chilli powder
1 teaspoon sugar
salt
1 × 400 g (14 oz) can tomatoes, chopped with the juice
450 g (1 lb) cooked crab meat (fresh, canned or frozen)

Preparation time: 10 minutes
Cooking time: 35–40 minutes

A mild curry, using crab meat, which is a popular ingredient for curries from the coastal areas of India. If using frozen crab meat, it should be allowed to thaw completely.

1. Heat the butter in a frying pan and fry the onion until just soft and transparent.
2. Add the garlic, coriander, nutmeg, chilli, sugar and salt. Stir and cook for a further 2–3 minutes.
3. Add the tomatoes and fry gently for 25–30 minutes, until reduced to a thick sauce.
4. Using a fork, break the crab meat into small chunks and gently stir into the sauce. Simmer very gently in the covered pan for 5–7 minutes. Serve with plain boiled rice, Sweetcorn curry (page 70), a green salad, poppadums, chutneys and pickles.

FROM THE LEFT: Karachala curry: Jhinga ne bholar marcha

JHINGA NE BHOLAR MARCHA (FRIED PRAWNS AND PEPPER)

100 g (4 oz) butter
1 large onion, peeled and finely chopped
2 tablespoons ground coriander
50 g (2 oz) desiccated coconut
450 g (1 lb) peeled prawns, thawed if frozen
1 teaspoon salt
1 teaspoon chilli powder
¼ teaspoon turmeric
1 large green pepper, cored, seeded and diced

Preparation time: 15 minutes
Cooking time: 25–30 minutes

1. Heat the butter in a large frying pan, add the onions and fry until just soft and transparent.
2. Add the coriander and coconut and fry for 2 minutes. Add the prawns and stir-fry until heated through, about 5–7 minutes.
3. Finally, add the remaining ingredients and stir-fry for a further 2–3 minutes. Serve immediately, accompanied by plain boiled rice

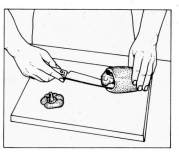
Loosening the core.

Tapping out seeds.

MEAT

KAJU GOSHT
(BEEF IN CASHEW NUTS)

450 g (1 lb) braising steak, cut into 2.5 cm (1 inch) cubes
100 g (4 oz) cashew nuts, finely ground
50 ml (2 fl oz) oil
½ quantity Basic curry sauce (page 8)
150 ml (¼ pint) soured cream
1 tablespoon plain flour
50 ml (2 fl oz) water
50 g (2 oz) cashew nuts, toasted, to garnish

Preparation time: 25 minutes
Cooking time: 1–1¼ hours
Oven: 180°C, 350°F, Gas Mark 4

The use of cashew nuts (kaju) in this medium curry together with soured cream creates a delicious flavour.

1. Arrange the beef in a casserole dish.
2. In a bowl, blend together the ground cashew nuts, oil, curry sauce, soured cream, flour and water.
3. Pour the mixture evenly over the meat. Cover and cook in a preheated oven for 1–1¼ hours or until the meat is tender. Stir once or twice during cooking.
4. Garnish with toasted nuts just before serving. Serve on a bed of plain boiled rice and accompany with a tomato and onion salad.

GOSHT (BEEF CURRY)

1 quantity Basic curry sauce (page 8)
150 ml (¼ pint) water
750 g (1½ lb) braising steak, cut into 2.5 cm (1 inch) cubes

Preparation time: 15 minutes
Cooking time: 1¼ hours

1. Place the curry sauce in a pan with the water and heat gently.
2. Add the meat and stir well. Cover and cook over a low heat for 1–1¼ hours until the meat is tender. Stir once or twice during cooking to prevent sticking. Serve with plain boiled rice, plain unsweetened yogurt, pickles and chutneys.

BROCCOLI GOSHT
(BEEF AND BROCCOLI)

100 g (4 oz) hard margarine
1 large onion, peeled and finely chopped
2 cloves garlic, peeled and creamed
450 g (1 lb) braising steak, cut into narrow strips
1 tablespoon ground coriander
1 teaspoon garam masala powder
1 teaspoon chilli powder
1 teaspoon mustard powder
salt
1 × 225 g (8 oz) can tomatoes, chopped with the juice
225 g (8 oz) broccoli spears, washed and separated

Preparation time: 30 minutes
Cooking time: 1 hour

The broccoli spears for this medium curry are used to add contrasting texture and colour. They should have tight, firm heads. Avoid those about to flower, as they break up easily and will disintegrate during the cooking. Frozen broccoli can be used in place of fresh, in which case, allow it to thaw completely and remove any excess liquid by draining thoroughly.

1. Melt the margarine in a large saucepan and fry the onion until lightly browned.
2. Add the garlic and fry for a further minute.
3. Add the strips of beef and fry until sealed on all sides. Reduce the heat then cover and cook the meat in its own juices until tender.
4. Add the coriander, garam masala, chilli, mustard and salt and stir-fry over a low heat for a few seconds.
5. Stir in the tomatoes and cook uncovered until almost dry.
6. Add the broccoli and stir-fry for a few minutes. Partly cover the pan and simmer until tender. Transfer to a serving dish, accompanied by plain boiled rice or chapatis.

FROM THE BOTTOM: Broccoli gosht: Kaju gosht

GOSHT BHAJI (BEEF IN SPINACH)

225 g (8 oz) butter
1 large onion, peeled and finely chopped
4 cloves garlic, peeled and creamed
750 g (1½ lb) braising steak, cut into 2.5 cm (1 inch) cubes
1 tablespoon garam masala powder
1 teaspoon chilli powder
300 ml (½ pint) water
1 × 450 g (1 lb) packet frozen spinach, thawed and
  chopped
salt

Preparation time: 20 minutes
Cooking time: 45 minutes

If you feel that 225 g (8 oz) butter is too much, reduce to 175 g (6 oz). The butter is essential for a rich, creamy flavour.

1. Melt the butter in a large pan over a medium heat and gently fry the onion until just soft and transparent.
2. Add the garlic and fry for a few seconds only, then add the meat, garam masala and chilli powder and fry until the meat is sealed on all sides.
3. Stir in the water. Reduce the heat then cover and cook until the meat is just tender.
4. Add the chopped spinach and salt. Cook for a further 20 minutes until most of the liquid has evaporated, and only the fat remains. Serve with chapatis and pickles. Doongri daal (page 58) makes a good accompaniment.

Variation:
1 kg (2 lb) fresh spinach or 450 g (1 lb) kale, washed, chopped and cooked with a little water and then liquidized, can be used in place of the frozen spinach.

SAHELU SHAAK (BEEF CURRY ALL IN ONE)

750 g (1½ lb) braising steak, cut into 2.5 cm (1 inch) cubes
2 large onions, peeled and finely chopped
2 cloves garlic, peeled and creamed
50 g (2 oz) piece of fresh ginger, peeled and chopped
2 tablespoons ground coriander
1 teaspoon ground cardamom
1 teaspoon chilli powder
1 teaspoon ground nutmeg
2 teaspoons sugar
1 teaspoon salt
120 ml (4 fl oz) oil
1 × 400 g (14 oz) can tomatoes, chopped with the juice

Preparation time: 25 minutes
Cooking time: 1–1¼ hours
Oven: 180°C, 350°F, Gas Mark 4

1. Arrange the beef in a casserole dish.
2. In a bowl mix together the remaining ingredients and stir well.
3. Pour the mixture evenly over the meat. Cover and cook in a preheated oven for 1–1¼ hours, stirring once or twice during the cooking time.
4. Serve with tomato and onion salad.

BOTI KEBAB

1 kg (2 lb) rump or fillet steak, cut into 5 cm (2 inch) cubes
4 cloves garlic, peeled and creamed
4 tablespoons oil
4 tablespoons lemon juice
1 teaspoon salt
2 green chillis, seeded and finely chopped
lemon quarters, to serve

Preparation time: 20 minutes, plus marinating
  overnight
Cooking time: 20–25 minutes
Oven: 220°C, 425°F, Gas Mark 7

1. Place the meat in a large bowl.
2. In a separate bowl mix the remaining ingredients and pour over the meat. Rub the mixture well into the meat. Cover tightly and leave overnight.
3. Before cooking, stir the marinated meat so that it is well coated with the spices. Thread the meat on to long metal skewers. Rest either end of the skewers on the 2 long edges of a narrow, oblong roasting tin, so that the juices collect in the tin.
4. Spoon the juices over the kebabs and cook on the top shelf in a preheated oven for 20–25 minutes, turning the kebabs once. Serve with lemon quarters.

CLOCKWISE FROM THE BOTTOM: Boti kebab; Gosht bhaji; Sahelu shaak

BHOLAR GOSHT (BEEF IN PEPPER)

50 g (2 oz) butter
450 g (1 lb) braising steak cut into narrow strips, about
    5 cm (2 inch) long
1 medium onion, peeled and chopped
50 g (2 oz) raisins
1 large green pepper, cored, seeded and cut into strips
50 g (2 oz) desiccated coconut
1 teaspoon chilli powder
1 teaspoon garam masala powder
1 teaspoon ground cinnamon
1 teaspoon salt

Preparation time: 25–30 minutes
Cooking time: 35–40 minutes

1. Heat the butter in a large frying pan. Add the beef, onion and raisins and stir-fry for about 5 minutes. Cover and cook over a low heat for 30–35 minutes until the meat is tender and there is no liquid left in the pan.
2. Add the remaining ingredients and stir-fry for a further 2–3 minutes. The finished dish should be dry and the pepper crunchy.
3. Serve with plain boiled rice, poppadoms and plain unsweetened yogurt.

BEEF HALEEM

25 g (1 oz) dried split peas
25 g (1 oz) dried red lentils
50 g (2 oz) whole wheat grain
50 g (2 oz) pearl barley
750 ml (1¼ pints) water
175 g (6 oz) butter
2 sticks cinnamon
4 whole cloves
2 large onions, peeled and finely chopped
50 g (2 oz) piece of fresh ginger, peeled and finely chopped
2 cloves garlic, peeled and creamed
1 tablespoon ground coriander
1 tablespoon fennel seeds, crushed
1 teaspoon ground cardamom
1 teaspoon chilli powder
750 g (1½ lb) braising steak, cut into 2.5 cm (1 inch) cubes
1 × 400 g (14 oz) can tomatoes, chopped with the juice
1 teaspoon sugar
salt

Preparation time: 45 minutes, plus soaking
    overnight
Cooking time: 1–1½ hours

MAGFALI GOSHT (BEEF IN PEANUT SAUCE)

450 g (1 lb) braising steak, cut into 2.5 cm (1 inch) cubes
1 medium onion, peeled and roughly chopped
50 ml (2 fl oz) oil
300 ml (½ pt) water
100 g (4 oz) fresh, unroasted peanuts, finely ground
2 tomatoes, skinned and roughly chopped
1 teaspoon chilli powder
1 teaspoon turmeric
salt

Preparation time: 20 minutes
Cooking time: about 1–1¼ hours

This is a Ugandan dish, where all the ingredients are cooked in a pan on top of the cooker. Peanuts are used unskinned in the recipe.

1. Place all the ingredients in a large saucepan and mix thoroughly over a medium heat. Bring to the boil, stirring occasionally.
2. Cover the pan, reduce the heat and simmer for about 45 minutes until the meat is tender. Remove the lid for the last 10 minutes and continue cooking until the sauce has thickened.

1. Soak the split peas, lentils, wheat grain and barley together overnight.
2. Drain and rinse the soaked pulses and grains. Drain again. Place 600 ml (1 pint) of the water in a saucepan. Bring to the boil and add the pulses and grains. Reduce the heat and simmer until tender and most of the liquid has been absorbed.
3. Heat the butter in a deep frying pan or large saucepan and add the cinnamon and cloves. Add the onions and fry until golden brown.
4. Stir in the ginger and garlic and fry for 5–7 seconds only, then add the remaining spices and fry for 2 minutes, stirring constantly to prevent burning.
5. Add the meat to the mixture and seal on all sides.
6. Finally, stir in the tomatoes, remaining water, sugar and salt. Cover, and cook for 1¼–1½ hours over a low heat until the meat is tender, stirring occasionally.
7. Add the cooked pulses, mix well, and heat through. Discard the cinnamon sticks before serving.

CLOCKWISE FROM THE FRONT: Beef haleem; Bholar gosht; Magfali gosht

FUNCY GOSHT
(BEEF IN RUNNER BEANS)

100 g (4 oz) butter
1 large onion, peeled and finely chopped
2 cloves garlic, peeled and creamed
1 tablespoon ground coriander
1 tablespoon garam masala powder
1 teaspoon chilli powder
1 teaspoon sugar
450 g (1 lb) braising steak, cut into 2.5 cm (1 inch) cubes
1 × 400 g (14 oz) can tomatoes, chopped with the juice
150 ml (¼ pint) water
salt
225 g (8 oz) runner beans, trimmed and sliced diagonally, in 2.5 cm (1 inch) lengths

Preparation time: 30 minutes
Cooking time: 1–1¼ hours

1. Melt the butter in a large pan over a medium heat and fry the onion until golden brown.
2. Add the garlic and fry for a few seconds, then add the spices and sugar, and stir for 1 minute.
3. Add the meat and seal on all sides, then stir in the tomatoes, water and salt. Reduce the heat. Cover and cook for 1–1½ hours until the meat is tender and only a little liquid remains.
4. Add the runner beans, stir well and cook gently until the beans are tender and most of the liquid has evaporated.

MINCE AND PEAS

450 g (1 lb) minced beef
1 large onion, peeled and finely chopped
2 cloves garlic, peeled and creamed
50 g (2 oz) piece of fresh ginger, peeled and finely chopped
1 tablespoon ground coriander
1 tablespoon garam masala powder
1 teaspoon chilli powder
1 × 400 g (14 oz) can tomatoes, chopped with the juice
1 × 225 g (8 oz) packet frozen minted peas
salt

Preparation time: 20 minutes
Cooking time: 30 minutes

1. Place the mince, onion, garlic, ginger and spices in a large pan over a medium heat and stir-fry until the fat is released from the meat.
2. Add the tomatoes, stir well and cook for 5 minutes.
3. Add the peas and salt, stir well, cover and cook over a low heat for 15 minutes.

KHEEMA NO PAUN
(MEAT LOAF WITH CURRY SAUCE)

750 g (1½ lb) minced beef
1 medium onion, peeled and minced
2 green chillis, seeded and finely chopped
1 tablespoon garam masala powder
1 tablespoon ground cumin
2 teaspoons salt
½ quantity Basic curry sauce (page 8)
150 ml (¼ pint) plain unsweetened yogurt
1 tablespoon plain flour
½ cucumber, diced into small cubes

Preparation time: 30 minutes
Cooking time: 1 hour
Oven: 180°C, 350°F, Gas Mark 4

This medium curry uses the familiar meat loaf but with an Indian interest. The traditional method is simplified, so that the loaf is wrapped in foil for baking. This method of cooking the meat loaf gives it a fine close-grained texture, making it very easy to slice. The delicious sauce with its tiny cubes of cucumber should be of a pouring consistency.

1. In a bowl mix together the mince, onion, chillis, garam masala, cumin and salt. Knead the mixture with the hands to blend the spices evenly through the mince.
2. Place the mince mixture on to an oiled surface and mould into a loaf shape.
3. Transfer the loaf on to a large piece of greased foil and wrap securely to retain the shape. Leave the foil at each end of the loaf turned upwards and slightly open. Place the loaf on to a baking sheet and bake in a preheated oven for 45 minutes.
4. Heat the curry sauce in a pan. Blend the yogurt with the flour and stir into the sauce. Bring to the boil, stirring constantly until thick.
5. Add the cucumber to the sauce and heat for a few seconds.
6. To serve, cut the loaf into fairly large slices, about 1 cm (½ inch) thick, allowing 2 slices per person. Then pour a little sauce over each slice. Fried courgettes (page 71) and Makai danaa (page 70) make good accompanying dishes. A green side salad could also be served.

CLOCKWISE FROM THE TOP: Kheema no paun; Kheema na gola; Funcy gosht

KHEEMA NA GOLA (MEATBALL CURRY)

750 g (1½ lb) minced beef
2 cloves garlic, peeled and creamed
1 teaspoon salt
1 green chilli, seeded and finely chopped
1 quantity Basic curry sauce (page 8)
300 ml (½ pint) water
sprigs of fresh coriander leaves, to garnish

Preparation time: 35 minutes
Cooking time: 30 minutes

1. Place the mince, garlic, salt and chilli in a bowl and mix in well using a kneading action.
2. Divide the mince into equal 16 portions and using a few drops of oil on the hands roll each one into a smooth ball.
3. Place the sauce and the water in a large pan and bring to the boil. Lower the heat and simmer gently.
4. Lower the golas (meatballs) into the simmering sauce; stir gently with a small-headed spoon to ensure they are coated with the sauce. Cover and cook for 25–30 minutes. Serve on a bed of plain boiled rice and garnish with coriander sprigs.

NARGISI KOFTA
(CURRIED MEATBALLS WITH EGGS)

750 g (1½ lb) minced beef
1 egg (size 1), beaten
50 g (2 oz) fresh breadcrumbs
4 cloves garlic, peeled and creamed
2 green chillis, seeded and finely chopped
2 teaspoons salt
4 small eggs, hard-boiled and shelled
1 quantity Basic curry sauce (page 8)
300 ml (½ pint) water
sprigs of fresh coriander leaves, to garnish

Preparation time: 35 minutes
Cooking time: 30 minutes

1. In a large bowl mix together the mince, beaten egg, breadcrumbs, garlic, chillis and salt, using a kneading action. Divide into 4 equal portions.
2. With oiled hands, shape each mince portion into a 13 cm (5 inch) round flat cake shape.
3. Place a hard-boiled egg in the centre of each shape, then mould the mince evenly around the egg making sure there are no thin areas. As the mince shrinks during cooking any thin areas will readily crack. Keep covered to prevent the surface drying.
4. Place the curry sauce and water into a medium-sized saucepan, and bring to the boil. Reduce the heat and simmer for 2–3 minutes.
5. Gently lower the koftas into the sauce, spooning the hot sauce on top if they are not quite submerged. Cover and cook gently for 25–30 minutes.
6. Cut each kofta in half and serve on a bed of saffron rice, garnished with coriander sprigs.

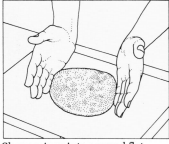

Shape mince into a round flat shape.

Place egg on mince.

Mould mince evenly around the egg.

KHEEMA BAINGAN (MINCE IN AUBERGINE)

450 g (1 lb) minced beef
1 large onion, peeled and chopped
2 cloves garlic, peeled and creamed
1 medium aubergine, cut into 5 cm (2 inch) lengths, 1 cm (½ inch) wide
1 tablespoon ground coriander
1 teaspoon ground ginger
2 teaspoons garam masala powder
1 × 400 g (14 oz) can tomatoes, chopped with the juice
1 teaspoon chilli powder
1 teaspoon sugar
salt

Preparation time: 20 minutes
Cooking time: about 30 minutes

1. Place the mince, onion and garlic in a large pan over a medium heat and stir-fry until the fat is released from the meat.
2. Add the aubergine, coriander, ginger and garam masala and stir-fry for a further few minutes.
3. Stir in the tomatoes, chilli, sugar and salt. Cover and cook over a low heat for 25–30 minutes.
4. Transfer to a heated platter and serve with rice.

KAALUM KEBAB (MINCE KEBAB)

750 g (1½ lb) minced beef
2 cloves garlic, peeled and creamed
2 green chillis, seeded and finely chopped
1 teaspoon salt
1 small lettuce, cleaned and shredded, to serve
sprigs of fresh coriander leaves, to garnish
lemon quarters, to garnish

Preparation time: 30 minutes
Cooking time: 15–20 minutes
Oven: 220°C, 425°F, Gas Mark 7

1. In a bowl, mix together all the ingredients and knead using the hands to blend evenly. Divide the mixture into 16 equal portions.
2. Rub a chopstick or utensil of similar size and thickness, with a little oil. Shape a portion of the meat around the pointed end of the chopstick to a length of about 10 cm (4 inches). Slide the kebab on to a greased baking sheet twirling the chopstick as the meat slides off. Repeat with remainder.
3. Bake on the top shelf of a preheated oven for 15–20 minutes.
4. Serve on a bed of shredded lettuce, garnished with coriander leaves and lemon quarters.

KHEEMA BHAJEE (MINCE AND SPINACH)

450 g (1 lb) minced beef
1 large onion, peeled and chopped
3–4 cloves garlic, peeled and creamed
1 tablespoon garam masala powder
1 × 400 g (14 oz) can tomatoes, chopped with the juice
2 teaspoons salt
1 teaspoon sugar
1 teaspoon chilli powder
1 × 450 g (1 lb) packet frozen spinach, thawed and finely chopped
50 g (2 oz) butter

Preparation time: 25–30 minutes
Cooking time: about 30–35 minutes

1. Place the mince, onion and garlic in a large pan and stir-fry over a medium heat, until the fat is released from the meat.
2. Add the garam masala and stir-fry for a few seconds, then add the tomatoes, salt, sugar and chilli powder and mix well.
3. Stir in the spinach, cover and cook over a low heat for 25 minutes.
4. Add the butter in small pieces and stir well. Cook for a further 5 minutes and serve with rice, pop-padums, plain unsweetened yogurt mixed with finely chopped tomato and pickles.

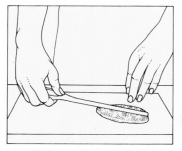

Lay oiled utensil across flattened mince shape.

Mould mince firmly around utensil to form kebab.

FROM THE BOTTOM: Kaalum kebab: Kheema baingan

PHOOLKOBI GOSHT (LAMB AND CAULIFLOWER)

100 g (4 oz) butter
1 large onion, peeled and chopped
1 clove garlic, peeled and creamed
50 g (2 oz) piece of fresh ginger, peeled and chopped
450 g (1 lb) lamb, cut into 2.5 cm (1 inch) cubes
1 × 400 g (14 oz) can tomatoes, chopped with the juice
150 ml (¼ pint) water
1 teaspoon sugar
1 teaspoon salt
1–1½ teaspoons chilli powder
1 tablespoon ground coriander
1 teaspoon ground cardamom
1 small cauliflower, washed and separated into small
    florets

Preparation time: 30 minutes
Cooking time: 1 hour

Cauliflower with its distinctive flavour adds an interesting texture to this medium curry and the florets can be left a little crunchy if preferred. Choose a cauliflower with white curds and no blemishes for the best flavour.

1. Heat the butter in a large pan and fry the onion until browned. Add the garlic and ginger and fry for a few seconds.
2. Add the meat and seal on all sides. Then mix in the remaining ingredients (except the cauliflower), adding chilli powder according to taste.
3. Cover and cook for about 55 minutes until the meat is tender and there is little liquid left in the pan.
4. Stir in the cauliflower, partly cover the pan and cook until the cauliflower is tender. Serve with plain boiled rice, Masoor daal tamatar (page 59) and pickles.

> To prepare the cauliflower, pull off the outside leaves and cut off the stem close under the head. The leaves and skin can be used for soup. Cut the florets off the central stalk and peel the thin skin off the stems with a knife. Cut a slit in any stems thicker than 5 mm (¼ inch) in diameter.

TOOYI TAMATAR GOSHT (LAMB WITH COCONUT CREAM AND TOMATOES)

750 g (1½ lb) lamb cut into 2.5 cm (1 inch) cubes
2 teaspoons salt
450 ml (¾ pint) water
2 sticks cinnamon
6 whole cloves
6 cardamom pods
1 large onion, peeled and quartered
1 large piece of fresh ginger, peeled and cut into slices
225 g (8 oz) coconut cream, grated
1 × 225 g (8 oz) can tomatoes, liquidized
sprigs of fresh coriander leaves, to garnish

Preparation time: 20 minutes
Cooking time: 1½ hours

This curry has a distinctive flavour of coconut with the tomato and yogurt sauce adding a tangy taste. The dish is cooked with whole spices, which are removed once the meat is cooked, making a mild-flavoured curry. A teaspoon of garam masala could be included to add an extra spicy touch.

1. Place the meat, salt, water, spices, onion and ginger in a large saucepan and bring to the boil, stirring occasionally.
2. Lower the heat and skim if necessary. Cover and cook for about 1 hour until the meat is just tender.
3. Strain the cooking liquid into a clean pan and discard the whole spices. Reserve the meat on a warmed plate.
4. Simmer the liquid, uncovered, until it has reduced to about 150 ml (¼ pint), then add the coconut cream and tomatoes. Stir constantly for about 5 minutes until the coconut has melted and the sauce has thickened.
5. Return the cooked meat to the sauce, cover and cook for a further 20–25 minutes until the meat is completely tender. If necessary a little water may be added to thin the sauce. Garnish with coriander leaves. Serve with saffron rice, Stuffed okra (page 68), a side salad and pickles.

FROM THE BOTTOM: Tooyi tamatar gosht; Phoolkobi gosht

DAHI WALA GOSHT (LAMB WITH CREAM AND YOGURT)

750 g (1½ lb) lamb cut into 2.5 cm (1 inch) cubes
2½ teaspoons salt
450 ml (¾ pint) water
1 teaspoon turmeric
1 teaspoon chilli powder
2 teaspoons ground cinnamon
1 large onion, peeled and finely chopped
2 cloves garlic, peeled and creamed
50 g (2 oz) piece of fresh ginger, peeled and chopped
100 g (4 oz) coconut cream, grated
150 ml (¼ pint) double cream
150 ml (¼ pint) plain unsweetened yogurt
2 sprigs fresh coriander leaves, chopped, to garnish

Preparation time: 20 minutes
Cooking time: 1½ hours

A mild curry with a subtle, spicy flavour. The method of cooking the meat is basically Ugandan, but spices have been added to the water to flavour the meat and stock. The extra ingredients mixed into the sauce give it a subtle, slightly tangy taste.

1. Place the meat, salt, water, spices, onion, garlic and ginger in a large pan and bring to the boil, stirring occasionally. Lower the heat and skim if necessary.
2. Cover and simmer for about 1¼ hours, until the meat is tender. Remove the lid for the last 15 minutes of cooking until most of the liquid has reduced. Stir occasionally during the cooking time.
3. Away from the heat add the coconut cream, double cream and yogurt. Stir constantly until the coconut cream has melted.
4. Heat gently for 10–15 minutes, without boiling. Sprinkle with chopped coriander and serve with chapatis and pickles.

FROM THE LEFT: Dahi wala gosht; Lamb curry in the oven

LAMB CURRY IN THE OVEN

750 g (1½ lb) lamb, cut into 2.5 cm (1 inch) cubes
1 large onion, peeled and finely chopped
2 cloves garlic, peeled and creamed
50 ml (2 fl oz) oil
1 tablespoon ground coriander
1 tablespoon mustard powder
1 teaspoon ground cardamom
1 teaspoon ground nutmeg
1 teaspoon chilli powder
2 teaspoons salt
2 teaspoons sugar
1 × 400 g (14 oz) can tomatoes, chopped with the juice

Preparation time: 20–25 minutes
Cooking time: 1¼ hours
Oven: 180°C, 350°F, Gas Mark 4

1. Arrange the meat in a casserole dish.
2. Mix the remaining ingredients in a bowl and stir well, then pour the mixture evenly over the meat.
3. Cover and cook for about 1¼ hours in a preheated oven, stirring once during cooking. Skim off any excess fat before serving with French beans and potato curry (page 77), and plain boiled rice.

LAMB CURRY

1 quantity Basic curry sauce (page 8)
300 ml (½ pint) water
750 g (1½ lb) lamb, cut into 2.5 cm (1 inch) cubes

Preparation time: 20 minutes
Cooking time: 1½ hours

This is a quick and easy, medium curry to make when time is short.

1. Place the curry sauce and water in a large pan and heat gently.
2. Add the meat, stir well, then cover and cook for about 1½ hours until the meat is tender, skimming off any excess fat before serving.
3. Serve with chapatis or plain boiled rice. Pickles and chutneys also add interest and a contrasting texture to the meat. To complete the meal, add a vegetable curry and a bean curry of your choice.

LEEK WALA GOSHT
(LAMB AND LEEK CURRY)

750 g (1½ lb) lamb cut into 2.5 cm (1 inch) cubes
1 large onion, peeled and finely chopped
2 cloves garlic, peeled and creamed
50 g (2 oz) fresh ginger, peeled and chopped
150 ml (¼ pint) plain unsweetened yogurt
1 tablespoon plain flour
1 × 225 g (8 oz) can tomatoes, chopped with the juice
50 ml (2 fl oz) oil
1 tablespoon garam masala powder
1 teaspoon chilli powder
2 teaspoons sugar
2 teaspoons salt
150 ml (¼ pint) water
450 g (1 lb) leeks, trimmed, washed and cut into 2.5 cm
    (1 inch) pieces

Preparation time: 25 minutes
Cooking time: 1½ hours
Oven: 180°C, 350°F, Gas Mark 4

1. Arrange the lamb in a large ovenproof dish.
2. In a bowl mix together the remaining ingredients, except the leeks, and pour the mixture evenly over the meat.
3. Cover and cook in a preheated oven for 1 hour, stirring once or twice during cooking.
4. Add the prepared leeks to the casserole and gently stir to cover the leeks with the sauce. Cook for a further 30 minutes, skimming off any excess fat before serving with saffron rice and a side salad.

LAMB KARANGA

100 g (4 oz) hard margarine
1 large onion, peeled and finely chopped
1 teaspoon cumin seeds, crushed
100 g (4 oz) fresh, unroasted peanuts, finely ground
1 tablespoon ground coriander
1 teaspoon chilli powder
1 × 225 g (8 oz) can tomatoes, chopped with the juice
1 teaspoon salt
750 g (1½ lb) lamb cut into 2.5 cm (1 inch) cubes
300 ml (½ pint) water
150 ml (¼ pint) soured cream, to serve

Preparation time: 25 minutes
Cooking time: about 1½ hours

TIL BHAJEE LAMB
(LAMB IN SESAME AND SPINACH)

100 g (4 oz) butter
2 large onions, peeled and chopped
150 g (6 oz) sesame seeds, ground
1 tablespoon ground coriander
1 tablespoon garam masala powder
1 teaspoon chilli powder
1 × 75 g (3 oz) can tomato purée
300 ml (½ pint) water
750 g (1½ lb) lamb cut into large cubes
1 × 450 g (1 lb) packet frozen spinach, thawed and
    chopped
2 teaspoons salt
1 teaspoon sugar

Preparation time: 25 minutes
Cooking time: about 1½ hours

A mild curry with an unusual sesame flavour.

1. Melt the butter in a large pan and fry the onions until just soft and transparent.
2. Add the sesame seeds and fry gently for 2–3 minutes, stirring constantly to prevent burning.
3. Add the coriander, garam masala and chilli powder and fry for 5–8 seconds, then add the remaining ingredients, and stir well. Cover and cook for 1–1½ hours over a low heat until the meat is tender. Serve with saffron rice, a side salad and poppadums.

This medium curry denotes a flavour of Ugandan cooking in the district of Toro.

1. Melt the margarine in a large pan over a medium heat and fry the onion until brown.
2. Add the cumin seeds and peanuts and fry for 2–3 minutes, then add the coriander and chilli powder and fry for a few seconds.
3. Stir in the tomatoes and salt. Fry for 4–5 minutes, then add the lamb and toss thoroughly in the mixture.
4. Blend in the water, then cover and cook for about 1½ hours over a low heat until the meat is tender.
5. Serve on a bed of rice with swirls of soured cream on top, accompanied by a selection of pickles and chutneys.

CLOCKWISE FROM THE FRONT: Lamb karanga; Leek wala gosht; Til bhajee lamb

TANDOORI LAMB CHOPS

4 tablespoons oil
50 ml (2 fl oz) plain unsweetened yogurt
1 teaspoon ground coriander
2 cloves garlic, peeled and creamed
1 teaspoon salt
1 teaspoon chilli powder
4 double lamb chops
1 small lettuce, washed, to serve
2 sprigs fresh coriander leaves, to garnish
lemon wedges, to garnish

Preparation time: 15 minutes, plus marinating
Cooking time: 20–25 minutes
Oven: 200°C, 400°F, Gas Mark 6

FROM THE LEFT: Tandoori lamb chops; Phoodina lamb

A hot curry, giving an exotic touch to lamb chops.

1. Place all the ingredients, except the chops, in a large bowl and mix thoroughly.
2. Place the chops in the bowl and using the hands, rub the mixture into the meat. Cover and leave to marinate for 4–6 hours.
3. Place the chops on a greased baking sheet or on a wire tray placed over a roasting tin and bake on the top shelf of a preheated oven for about 20–25 minutes. Turn the chops once during the cooking time.
4. Serve on a bed of lettuce and garnish with coriander sprigs and lemon wedges.

PHOODINA LAMB
(MINTY LAMB CURRY)

100 g (4 oz) butter
1 large onion, peeled and finely chopped
1 tablespoon ground coriander
1 teaspoon ground cardamom
1 teaspoon fennel seeds, crushed
1 × 400 g (14 oz) can tomatoes, chopped with the juice
1 teaspoon salt
1 teaspoon sugar
1 tablespoon mint sauce
150 ml (¼ pint) water
450 g (1 lb) lamb cut into 2.5 cm (1 inch) cubes
sprigs of fresh mint, to garnish

Preparation time: 25 minutes
Cooking time: about 1–1½ hours

This mild curry is created from two ingredients which traditionally go together in Western dishes. The mint is combined with other spices to give a unique flavour to the lamb.

1. Melt the butter in a large saucepan and fry the onion until golden brown.
2. Add the coriander, cardamom and fennel seeds and fry for a few seconds, stirring constantly to prevent burning.
3. Add the tomatoes, salt, sugar and mint sauce and cook for 5 minutes.
4. Stir in the water and meat and mix well with the sauce. Cover and cook for about 1–1½ hours over a low heat until the meat is tender.
5. Serve with plain boiled rice and accompany with a vegetable curry, such as Baingan batata (page 64).

PORK DHANSAK

450 g (1 lb) pie pork or pork steak, cut into 2.5–4 cm (1–1½ inch) pieces
100 g (4 oz) dried red lentils, soaked for a few hours and drained
1 large onion, peeled and finely chopped
2 cloves garlic, peeled and creamed
85 ml (3 fl oz) oil
2 tablespoons ground coriander
1 teaspoon garam masala powder
1 teaspoon ground cardamom
1 teaspoon ground white pepper
1 teaspoon salt
2 teaspoons sugar
1 × 400 g (14 oz) can tomatoes, chopped with the juice
150 ml (¼ pint) water

Preparation time: 20–25 minutes, plus soaking
Cooking time: 1¼–1½ hours
Oven: 180°C, 350°F, Gas Mark 4

1. Trim off the excess fat from the meat and arrange in a casserole dish.
2. In a bowl combine the remaining ingredients and pour evenly over the meat.
3. Cover and cook in a preheated oven for 1¼–1½ hours, stirring once during the cooking time.
4. Stir thoroughly before serving with saffron rice. Chapatis, pickles and chutneys also go well with this dish.

PORK AND PEACHES

4 medium pork steaks
1 × 400 g (14 oz) can peach slices, drained and liquid reserved
1 large onion, peeled and finely chopped
1 clove garlic, peeled and creamed
50 ml (2 fl oz) oil
1 tablespoon ground coriander
1 tablespoon mustard powder
1 tablespoon fennel seeds, crushed
1 × 225 g (8 oz) can tomatoes, chopped with the juice
1 teaspoon turmeric
1 teaspoon chilli powder
salt

Preparation time: 25 minutes
Cooking time: 1–1¼ hours
Oven: 180°C, 350°F, Gas Mark 4

PORK VATANA (PORK AND HARICOT BEANS)

450 g (1 lb) pie pork or pork steak, cut into 2.5–4 cm (1–1½ inch) pieces
1 large onion, peeled and chopped
2 cloves garlic, peeled and creamed
1 tablespoon ground coriander
1 tablespoon mustard powder
1 teaspoon ground cinnamon
1 teaspoon salt
1 teaspoon sugar
1 × 225 g (8 oz) can tomatoes, chopped with the juice
50 ml (2 fl oz) oil
1 × 425 g (15 oz) can haricot beans, drained and liquid reserved
1 green pepper, cored, seeded and sliced, to garnish

Preparation time: 25 minutes
Cooking time: 1–1¼ hours
Oven: 180°C, 350°F, Gas Mark 4

1. Arrange the meat in a casserole dish.
2. In a bowl mix together the onion, garlic, spices, salt, sugar, tomatoes, oil and liquid from the beans.
3. Pour this mixture evenly over the meat, cover and cook for 1 hour in a preheated oven until the meat is tender.
4. Stir in the drained beans and cook for a further 15 minutes. Serve with chapatis and green pepper slices, to garnish.

1. Arrange the pork steaks in a casserole dish.
2. In a bowl mix together the liquid from the can of peaches, onion, garlic, oil, coriander, mustard, fennel, tomatoes, turmeric, chilli and salt. Pour this mixture evenly over the steaks.
3. Cover and cook in a preheated oven for 45 minutes.
4. Remove from the oven and gently stir the sauce. Arrange the peach slices attractively on top of the steaks. Cover and complete the cooking time.
5. Serve with plain boiled rice and a side salad.

CLOCKWISE FROM THE FRONT: Pork and peaches; Pork dhansak; Pork vatana

BHOONA GOSHT (ROAST PORK WITH CURRY SAUCE)

1½–1¾ kg (3–4 lb) leg of pork
2 cloves garlic, peeled and creamed
2 tablespoons oil
1 tablespoon fennel seeds, ground
1 tablespoon salt
½ quantity Basic curry sauce (page 8)
150 ml (¼ pint) plain unsweetened yogurt
150 ml (¼ pint) single cream
2 × 150 g (5 oz) cans apple sauce
8 whole cloves, crushed
fennel leaves and bulb, sliced, to garnish

Preparation time: 15–20 minutes
Cooking time: 1½–2 hours
Oven: 190°C, 375°F, Gas Mark 5

1. Using a sharp knife, slash the surface of the meat all over.
2. In a bowl mix together the garlic, oil, fennel and salt and rub all over the meat.
3. Transfer the meat into a roasting tin and roast in a preheated oven for 1½–2 hours. Baste once or twice during cooking.
4. Place the curry sauce in a pan with the remaining ingredients and heat gently without boiling, then pour into a warmed sauceboat.
5. Place the meat on a large serving dish, garnish with fennel and serve with the sauce. Funcy shaak (page 77) and plain boiled rice would go well with this dish.

TANDOORI PORK CHOPS

4 large pork chump chops
2 cloves garlic, peeled and creamed
4 tablespoons oil
1 small can pineapple rings, drained (reserve 4
    tablespoons of the juice)
1 tablespoon mustard powder
1 tablespoon paprika
1 teaspoon salt
1 teaspoon brown sugar
1 small lettuce, cleaned and shredded, to serve

**Preparation time: 25 minutes, plus marinating
    overnight**
Cooking time: about 45 minutes
Oven: 220°C, 424°F, Gas Mark 7

1. Trim excess fat from the chops, and place in a large mixing bowl.
2. In a separate bowl mix together the garlic, oil, pineapple juice, mustard, paprika, salt and sugar.
3. Pour the mixture over the chops and rub well into the meat. Cover and leave overnight to marinate.
4. Before cooking, rub the chops with the marinade and place on a wire tray over a roasting tin.
5. Bake in a preheated oven one shelf above the centre. Cook for 20–25 minutes, turning the chops once during cooking.
6. Remove the dish. Place the pineapple rings attractively on each chop, return to the oven and bake for a further 10–15 minutes. Serve on a bed of shredded lettuce, accompanied by chapatis or naan, plain unsweetened yogurt and a mixed salad.

FROM THE LEFT: Bhoona gosht; Tandoori pork chops

PORK ANANAS (PORK IN PINEAPPLE)

100 g (4 oz) butter
1 large onion, peeled and finely chopped
1 rounded teaspoon garam masala powder
1 rounded teaspoon ground cinnamon
1 rounded teaspoon ground ginger
1 rounded teaspoon chilli powder
1 rounded teaspoon garlic powder
1 × 400 g (14 oz) can tomatoes, chopped with the juice
150 ml (¼ pint) water
1 × 300 g (11 oz) can pineapple pieces, plus juice
750 g (1½ lb) pie pork or pork steak, cut into 2.5–4 cm
   (1–1½ inch) pieces and trimmed
salt

Preparation time: 25 minutes
Cooking time: 1½ hours

The pineapple provides the main accent in this medium-flavoured, fruity curry.

1. Heat the butter in a large pan and fry the onion until just transparent.
2. Add the spices and garlic powder and fry for a few seconds, stirring constantly to prevent burning.
3. Stir in the tomatoes and fry for 5–7 minutes.
4. Add the remaining ingredients, and stir well. Cover and cook over a gentle heat for 1½ hours until the pork is tender. Stir occasionally during the cooking time. Serve together with Meat loaf with curry sauce (page 22), chapatis and a green salad.

Variation:
Canned pineapple is used as it is a handy, storecupboard item. Fresh fruit can also be used and the seasoning adjusted with a little sugar. To prepare a fresh pineapple, place the whole fruit on its side, then slice off the top and bottom. Stand the fruit upright and using a bread knife or serrated knife, cut off the skin with a sawing movement. Remove any remaining 'eyes'. Slice the fruit and remove the hard, centre core, then cut into pieces.

To choose a pineapple that is ripe for eating, first sniff the stem end. If there is no aroma, it is not ready. A ripe pineapple should have a sweet smell, feel heavy for its size, and it should be easy to pull out one of the leaves.

PORK SAFARJAN (PORK IN APPLE AND YOGURT)

4 medium pork steaks
1 large onion, peeled and minced
1 large apple, peeled, cored and minced
50 g (2 oz) raisins
50 ml (2 fl oz) oil
150 ml (¼ pint) plain unsweetened yogurt
50 ml (2 fl oz) water
1 tablespoon plain flour
1 tablespoon ground coriander
1 tablespoon mustard powder
1 teaspoon chilli powder
1 teaspoon salt
2 teaspoons sugar

Preparation time: 20–25 minutes
Cooking time: 1–1¼ hours
Oven: 180°C, 350°F, Gas Mark 4

A new variation on the traditional Sunday theme of roast pork and apple. This medium curry is quick to prepare and simple to cook, as all the ingredients are baked together in the oven.

1. Arrange the pork steaks in a casserole dish.
2. In a bowl blend the remaining ingredients together and pour evenly over the meat.
3. Cover and cook in a preheated oven for 1–1¼ hours, stirring once during the cooking time.
4. Serve on a bed of rice and accompany with a side salad and pickles. Three bean curry (page 54) would also go well with this dish.

TIL GOORDA (SESAME KIDNEYS)

100 g (4 oz) butter
1 large onion, peeled and minced
100 g (4 oz) sesame seeds, finely ground
1 × 225 g (8 oz) can tomatoes, chopped with the juice
150 ml (¼ pint) water
1 teaspoon garam masala powder
1 tablespoon lemon juice
1 tablespoon sugar
salt
350 g (12 oz) lamb's kidneys, halved and cored

Preparation time: 20 minutes
Cooking time: 30–35 minutes

SUKKEE KALEJEE (GRILLED LIVER)

50 ml (2 fl oz) oil
1 tablespoon ground cumin
1 teaspoon garlic powder
1 teaspoon chilli powder
2 teaspoons salt
1 tablespoon tomato purée
1 tablespoon brown sugar
1 tablespoon lemon juice
4 portions lamb's liver, about 175 g (6 oz) each, each piece sliced in 2
1 small lettuce, cleaned and shredded, to serve
1 lime, sliced, to garnish

Preparation time: 10 minutes, plus marinating
Cooking time: about 20 minutes

This is a dry dish, which can be used as an accompaniment to other meat or vegetable curries or on its own as a snack. It also makes a good starter, when served on a bed of lettuce, with lemon or lime quarters.

1. Place all the ingredients except the liver into a large bowl and mix thoroughly.
2. Spread the mixture over the liver until every piece is completely coated. Cover and leave to marinate for 30 minutes.
3. Before cooking, toss the liver well in the mixture.
4. Place the liver on the rack in the grill pan and grill each side for 10 minutes. Serve immediately on a bed of shredded lettuce, garnished with slices of lime.

This mild curry, when served with plain boiled rice, makes a warming lunchtime meal. Ground sesame is a popular ingredient in Ugandan cooking and gives a good, strong flavour to the kidneys.

1. Melt the butter in a pan and fry the onion until soft and transparent.
2. Add the sesame seeds and fry for 1–2 minutes.
3. Stir in the tomatoes, water, garam masala, lemon juice, sugar and salt, and cook for 10 minutes.
4. Add the kidneys to the sauce and stir well. Cover and cook over a low heat for about 20 minutes until tender. Make sure not to overcook the kidneys as they will toughen if cooked longer than necessary.
5. Serve with saffron rice and plain yogurt sprinkled with grated lime, for a light lunch.

CLOCKWISE FROM THE FRONT: Til goorda; Sukee kalejee

POULTRY

APRICOT KUKU
(CHICKEN IN APRICOTS)

1 × 1¾ kg (4 lb) chicken, skinned and jointed
50 ml (2 fl oz) oil
2 large onions, peeled and finely chopped
2 cloves garlic, peeled and creamed
2 tablespoons ground coriander
1 teaspoon ground cardamom
1½ teaspoons chilli powder
1 teaspoon sugar
salt
1 × 400 g (14 oz) can tomatoes, chopped with the juice
1 × 400 g (14 oz) can apricots, drained and half the liquid
  reserved

Preparation time: 30–35 minutes
Cooking time: 1½ hours
Oven: 180°C, 325°F, Gas Mark 4

This is a medium, fruity curry. The apricots should
be fairly firm, so that they retain their shape during
cooking.

1. Arrange the chicken joints in a large casserole
dish.
2. In a bowl mix together the remaining ingredients,
adding salt to taste and half the fruit. Pour the
mixture evenly over the chicken. Cover and cook in a
preheated oven for 1 hour.
3. Remove the casserole from the oven and gently
spoon the sauce over the chicken pieces. Arrange the
remaining fruit attractively on the chicken, then
cover and cook for a further 30 minutes or until the
chicken is tender.
4. Serve with plain boiled rice, accompanied by
Baingan matar (page 75) and Three bean curry (page
54).

Fresh apricots may be used when in season, in
place of the canned ones, but they have to be
sweetened. Place 450 g (1 lb) fresh apricot
halves in a pan with 300 ml (½ pint) water and
2 tablespoons sugar. Poach gently until tender
then remove apricots from the pan and reduce
the liquid to 150 ml (¼ pint).

JUGI WALI MOORGI
(CHICKEN IN PEANUT SAUCE)

1 × 1¾ kg (4 lb) chicken, skinned and jointed
2 large onions, peeled and finely chopped
2 cloves garlic, peeled and creamed
100 g (4 oz) peanut butter
1 × 400 g (14 oz) can tomatoes, chopped with the juice
1 teaspoon ground cinnamon
1 tablespoon ground cumin
1 teaspoon chilli powder
2 teaspoons paprika
2 teaspoons brown sugar
1 teaspoon salt
2 tablespoons lemon juice
1–2 sprigs fresh coriander leaves, to garnish

Preparation time: 30 minutes
Cooking time: 1–1½ hours
Oven: 180°C, 325°F, Gas Mark 4

The use of peanut butter together with the other
spices in this medium curry gives it a delicious,
nutty flavour. It is quickly prepared and easy to cook.
If chicken joints are bought instead of a whole
chicken, make sure they are skinned.

1. Using a sharp knife, make a few slanting cuts on
the fleshy part of the chicken joints, then arrange
them in a casserole dish.
2. In a bowl, mix together the remaining ingredients
and pour the sauce evenly over the chicken.
3. Cover and cook in a preheated oven for about 1–
1½ hours or until tender. Stir the sauce and baste the
chicken joints once during the cooking time.
4. Serve with plain boiled rice and garnish with
coriander sprigs. To accompany this dish serve Khat
malai phoolkobi (page 70).

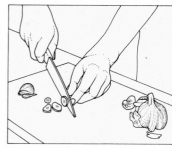
Slicing the garlic.

Crushing with salt.

FROM THE BOTTOM: Jugu wali moorgi; Apricot kuku

DAAL CHICKEN (CHICKEN IN LENTILS)

1 × 1½ kg (3¼ lb) chicken, skinned and jointed
1 quantity Basic curry sauce (page 8)
300 ml (½ pint) water
100 g (4 oz) dried red lentils, soaked overnight and
    drained

**Preparation time: 20 minutes, plus soaking
    overnight**
Cooking time: 1–1¼ hours

1. Using a sharp knife, make a few slanting cuts on
the fleshy part of the chicken joints and reserve.
2. Place the curry sauce and water in a large pan and
bring to the boil. Reduce the heat and lower in the
chicken pieces. Stir until well coated with the sauce.
Cover and cook for 35 minutes.
3. Stir in the drained lentils, then cover and cook
over a medium heat until the chicken is tender and
the lentils are cooked having formed a thick sauce,
about 30 minutes. Stir once or twice during cooking
to prevent sticking.
4. Serve with saffron rice and Cauliflower rangeen
(page 70).

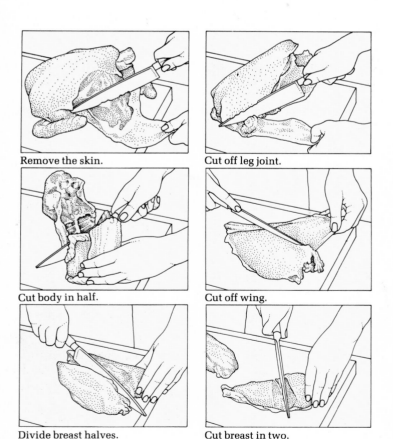

Remove the skin.

Cut off leg joint.

Cut body in half.

Cut off wing.

Divide breast halves.

Cut breast in two.

PISI'S CHICKEN CURRY

1 × 1½ kg (3¼ lb) chicken, skinned and jointed
100 g (4 oz) butter
1 large onion, peeled and chopped
1 tablespoon ground coriander
1 tablespoon garam masala powder
1 teaspoon chilli powder
8 tomatoes, finely chopped
300 ml (½ pint) water
1 teaspoon turmeric
salt
2 tablespoons chopped fresh coriander leaves
sprigs of fresh coriander leaves, to garnish

Preparation time: 30 minutes
Cooking time: 1–1½ hours

1. Using a sharp knife, make a few slanting cuts in the fleshy part of the chicken joints and set aside.
2. Heat the butter in a large pan and fry the onion until browned.
3. Add the ground coriander, garam masala and chilli powder and fry for a few seconds, stirring constantly. Add the tomatoes and fry for 5–7 minutes.
4. Stir in the water, turmeric and salt and blend thoroughly. Bring the sauce to the boil, then add the chicken pieces and coat with the sauce. Lower the heat, then cover and cook until tender.
5. Add the fresh coriander, stir and cook for a further 5–7 minutes. Serve with plain yogurt mixed with finely diced cucumber. Garnish with coriander sprigs.

MOORGI (CHICKEN CURRY)

1 × 1½ kg (3¼ lb) chicken, skinned and jointed
1 quantity Basic curry sauce (page 8)
85 ml (3 fl oz) water

Preparation time: 15 minutes
Cooking time: 1–1¼ hours

1. Using a sharp knife make a few slanting cuts on the fleshy part of the chicken joints and set aside.
2. Place the curry sauce and water in a large pan and heat gently. Add the chicken joints and stir until evenly coated with the sauce. Cover and cook over a low heat for 1–1¼ hours or until tender.
3. Serve with Kobi batata (page 69), saffron rice and a mixed salad.

FROM THE LEFT: Daal chicken; Pisi's chicken curry

CHICKEN IN COCONUT CREAM

4 large chicken breasts, skinned
200 ml (⅓ pint) water
1 medium onion, peeled and quartered
2 cloves garlic, peeled and sliced
50 g (2 oz) piece of fresh ginger, peeled and sliced
salt
175 g (6 oz) coconut cream, grated or chopped
½ teaspoon turmeric
2 tablespoons lemon juice
lemon quarters, to garnish

Preparation time: 25–30 minutes
Cooking time: 1–1¼ hours

1. Place the chicken breasts in a large pan together with the water, onion, garlic, ginger and salt. Cover and cook until the chicken is tender.
2. Using a slotted draining spoon, lift the chicken breasts on to a plate. Cover and keep hot.
3. Strain the cooking liquid into a separate pan and discard the spices. Simmer the liquid gently and add the coconut cream, turmeric and lemon juice. Stir continuously, until the coconut cream has melted and the sauce has thickened.
4. Return the chicken breasts to the sauce and cook for a further 10–15 minutes.
5. Serve garnished with the lemon quarters and accompanied by plain boiled rice and a green side salad with a vinaigrette dressing.

POT ROAST CHICKEN

50 g (2 oz) butter
50 g (2 oz) oil
2 large onions, peeled and sliced
2 cloves garlic, peeled and creamed
50 g (2 oz) piece of fresh ginger, peeled and finely chopped
1 tablespoon garam masala powder
1 tablespoon ground coriander
8 tomatoes, skinned and chopped
2 green chillis, seeded and chopped
salt
1 × 1½ kg (3–3½ lb) chicken, skinned and giblets removed
sprigs of fresh coriander leaves, to garnish

Preparation time: 25–30 minutes
Cooking time: 1½ hours
Oven: 180°C, 325°F, Gas Mark 4

1. Heat the butter and oil in a large frying pan and fry the onions until brown.
2. Add the garlic and ginger and fry for 1 minute. Then add the garam masala and coriander and fry for a further minute. Stir in the tomatoes, chillis and salt and fry for 2–3 minutes.
3. Place the whole chicken in the pan and seal all over, basting thoroughly with the mixture.
4. Place in a casserole. Cover and cook in a pre-heated oven until tender, basting once or twice. Uncover for the last 20 minutes to brown.
5. Serve garnished with coriander sprigs and hand the sauce round separately.

FROM THE LEFT: Pot roast chicken; Chicken tikka

CHICKEN TIKKA

1 × 1½ kg (3–3½ lb) chicken, skinned and jointed
150 ml (¼ pint) plain unsweetened yogurt
85 ml (3 fl oz) oil
1 medium onion, peeled and minced
4 cloves garlic, peeled and creamed
1 tablespoon cumin seeds, crushed
2 green chillis, seeded and chopped
5–6 sprigs fresh coriander leaves, chopped
salt
1 teaspoon turmeric

**Preparation time: 45 minutes, plus marinating
  overnight
Cooking time: 35–45 minutes
Oven: 220°C, 424°F, Gas Mark 7**

1. Using a sharp knife, make a few slanting cuts on
the fleshy part of the joints and place them in a
covered container.
2. In a bowl, mix together the remaining ingredients.
Pour the mixture over the chicken and rub it well
into the flesh. Cover and leave to marinate overnight.
3. Before cooking, rub the marinade into the chick-
en, then place the joints in a greased roasting tin or
on a wire tray placed over a roasting tin.
4. Roast in a preheated oven on one shelf above the
centre. Cook until tender and the chicken appears
slightly charred.
5. Serve with a green salad and chapatis or naan.

BADAMI TURKEY
(TURKEY IN ALMOND SAUCE)

4 turkey fillets, about 150 g (5 oz) each, skinned
75 g (3 oz) butter
1 teaspoon garlic powder
1 teaspoon salt
1 medium onion, peeled and minced
100 g (4 oz) ground almonds
150 ml (¼ pint) soured cream
about 150 ml (¼ pint) single cream
1 tablespoon garam masala powder
3–4 sprigs fresh coriander leaves, chopped

**Preparation time: 25 minutes
Cooking time: 1 hour
Oven: 180°C, 350°F, Gas Mark 4**

1. Place a large piece of foil in a roasting tin and
arrange the turkey breasts on the foil.
2. Divide 25 g (1 oz) of the butter between each
turkey breast, and sprinkle liberally with garlic
powder and salt.
3. Fold the foil edges inwards to make a loose
parcel. Cook in a preheated oven for 1 hour.
preheated oven and cook for 1 hour.
4. Heat the remaining butter in a pan and fry the
onion gently until soft and transparent.
5. Add the ground almonds and fry for 2–3 minutes.
6. Blend in the soured cream and 150 ml (¼ pint)
single cream. Heat through gently without boiling
adding extra cream to thin, if necessary.
7. To serve, pour sauce over the meat and sprinkle
with garam masala and chopped coriander.

MASALA TURKEY DRUMSTICKS

8 large turkey drumsticks, skinned
120 ml (4 fl oz) oil
2 teaspoons salt
4 tablespoons paprika
2 teaspoons garlic powder
1 × 425 g (15 oz) can sweetcorn, drained
lemon quarters, to garnish

**Preparation time: 10 minutes, plus marinating
  overnight**
Cooking time: 30–35 minutes
Oven: 220°C, 425°F, Gas Mark 7

Turkey has become very popular since the 1970s. It can now be bought in many different cuts and sizes. Choose large turkey drumsticks for this mild recipe to make satisfying portions. Smaller drumsticks could be used to make a starter, served with lemon quarters and a plain unsweetened yogurt.

1. Using a sharp knife, make 2 slanting cuts on each drumstick and place in a covered container. Add the remaining ingredients, except the sweetcorn, to the drumsticks and rub well, making sure the drumsticks are covered with the spices. Cover and leave to marinate overnight.
2. Before cooking, rub the turkey with the spices and arrange in a greased roasting tin or on a wire tray placed over the tin. Roast in a preheated oven for 30–35 minutes. Alternatively, place the drumsticks on the wire tray in the grill pan and cook under a preheated grill. Turn the drumsticks several times to ensure even cooking.
3. Transfer the cooked drumsticks on to a serving dish and keep hot.
4. Add the sweetcorn to the roasting pan with the oil and any remaining juices from the turkey and heat through, stirring well. Spoon the sweetcorn around the drumsticks and garnish with lemon quarters. Serve immediately with naan, plain yogurt and a side salad.

To skin a drumstick, lift the skin at the fattest part with one hand and hold on to the flesh with the other. Pull the skin down firmly, as far as it will go, then cut it off with a sharp knife at the ankle joint. To prevent the ends of the drumsticks becoming scorched during cooking, wrap them in foil. To serve, cover the ends with paper cutlet frills, if liked.

EGGS & PULSES

INDAA NU SHAAK (EGG CURRY)

1 quantity Basic curry sauce (page 8)
150 ml (¼ pint) water
8 eggs (size 1 or 2), hard-boiled and shelled
freshly boiled rice, to serve
sprigs of fresh coriander leaves, to garnish

Preparation time: 10 minutes
Cooking time: 10 minutes

1. Place the sauce in a pan with the water and bring to the boil.
2. Reduce the heat and gently lower in the eggs. Cover and simmer for 10 minutes.
3. To serve, pour the sauce over the rice. Cut the eggs in half and arrange on top of the sauce. Garnish with coriander sprigs and serve with a green salad and chutneys.

COPRA INDAA (EGGS IN COCONUT SAUCE)

1 fresh coconut, liquid drained and reserved
250–300 ml (8–10 fl oz) water
2 tablespoons oil
1 green chilli, seeded and finely chopped
5 whole cloves, crushed
1 small onion, peeled and finely chopped
1 clove garlic, peeled and creamed
1 teaspoon ground coriander
1 teaspoon ground cinnamon
2 tablespoons chopped fresh coriander leaves
½ teaspoon turmeric
salt
8 hard-boiled eggs, size 1, shelled and cut in 4 lengthways

Preparation time: 1 hour
Cooking time: 20–25 minutes

1. Break up the coconut with a hammer and remove the white flesh. Liquidize the flesh, liquid and water together to make a smooth sauce.
2. Heat the oil in a pan, add the remaining ingredients, except the eggs, and fry gently for 5 minutes.
3. Add the coconut mixture and cook for 15 minutes, stirring gently. Pour into a warm serving dish and arrange the egg quarters on top.

KASHMIRI EGGS

75 g (3 oz) butter
1 large onion, peeled and sliced
4 medium potatoes, peeled and thickly sliced
8 eggs (size 1 or 2), beaten
1 teaspoon freshly ground black pepper
salt

Preparation time: 15–20 minutes
Cooking time: 25–30 minutes

1. Heat the butter in a large frying pan, then add the onion and potatoes and fry until tender. Turn the potato slices frequently to ensure even cooking and browning.
2. Add the beaten eggs, pepper and salt to the pan and cook until the egg has set.

EGG MASALA

8 eggs (size 1 or 2)
5–6 sprigs fresh coriander leaves, chopped
1 medium onion, peeled and minced
4 medium tomatoes, chopped
1 tablespoon ground coriander
1 teaspoon chilli powder
salt
50 g (2 oz) butter

Preparation time: 20 minutes
Cooking time: 10–15 minutes

1. Break the eggs into a bowl and beat well. Add the remaining ingredients, except the butter, and mix well.
2. Heat the butter in a frying pan and add the egg mixture. Stir-fry, breaking up any lumps of cooked eggs, until the mixture resembles dry scrambled eggs.
3. Serve as a starter with triangles of toasted bread or as a light supper dish accompanied by a green salad.

FROM THE BOTTOM: Indaa nu shaak; Egg masala

THREE BEAN CURRY

100 g (4 oz) butter
2 medium onions, peeled and finely chopped
3 cloves garlic, peeled and creamed
1 tablespoon ground coriander
1 teaspoon garam masala powder
1 teaspoon chilli powder
1 × 400 g (14 oz) can tomatoes, chopped with the juice
salt
1 teaspoon sugar
1 × 425 g (15 oz) can butter beans, drained
1 × 425 g (15 oz) can kidney beans, drained
1 × 425 g (15 oz) can haricot beans or cannellini beans,
   drained
5−6 sprigs fresh coriander leaves, chopped, to garnish

Preparation time: 25 minutes
Cooking time: 30−35 minutes

A simply prepared, medium curry. All the beans should be easily obtainable in large supermarkets.

1. Heat the butter in a pan, add the onions and fry until light golden brown.
2. Add the garlic and fry for a few seconds only then add the coriander, garam masala and chilli powder and stir-fry for a few seconds.
3. Stir in the tomatoes, salt and sugar. Reduce the heat and cook for 10 minutes.
4. Carefully add the drained beans, stir thoroughly then cover and heat gently.
5. Serve garnished with the chopped coriander. Kobi gaajer (page 68) and plain boiled rice or chapatis make good accompanying dishes, together with pickles and a side salad.

BUTTER BEANS IN SESAME

120 ml (4 fl oz) oil
1 teaspoon cumin seeds
1 large onion, peeled and chopped
100 g (4 oz) sesame seeds, finely ground
1 tablespoon ground coriander
1 × 400 g (14 oz) can tomatoes, chopped with the juice
2 teaspoons salt
2 teaspoons sugar
1 teaspoon chilli powder
1 teaspoon turmeric
2 × 425 g (15 oz) cans butter beans, drained
2 sprigs fresh coriander leaves, chopped, to garnish

Preparation time: 20 minutes
Cooking time: 25–30 minutes

Ground sesame adds a delicious flavour and a variety of texture to this medium curry.

1. Heat the oil in a pan, add the cumin seeds and fry until they begin to crackle.
2. Add the onion and fry until soft and transparent.
3. Add the ground sesame seeds and fry for 3–5 minutes, then add the ground coriander and fry for a further minute.
4. Stir in the tomatoes, salt, sugar, chilli powder and turmeric. Mix well and cook the sauce for 3–5 minutes.
5. Add the drained beans and stir carefully until well coated with the sauce. Simmer until the beans are thoroughly hot. Sprinkle with chopped coriander and serve with chapatis. Cauliflower rangeen (page 70) and any of the meat curries make a good accompaniment.

FROM THE LEFT: Three bean curry; Butter beans in sesame

JANJADO KARANGA (KIDNEY BEANS IN PEANUT SAUCE)

120 ml (4 fl oz) oil
2 teaspoons cumin seeds
100 g (4 oz) fresh unroasted peanuts, ground
1 large onion, peeled and chopped
1 × 400 g (14 oz) can tomatoes, chopped with the juice
1 tablespoon ground coriander
1 teaspoon chilli powder
1 teaspoon salt
1 teaspoon sugar
2 × 425 g (15 oz) cans kidney beans, drained, reserving the liquid from 1 can only
3–4 sprigs fresh coriander leaves, chopped, to garnish

Preparation time: 25–30 minutes
Cooking time: 25–30 minutes

1. Heat the oil in a frying pan, and fry the cumin seeds until they begin to crackle.
2. Add the ground peanuts and fry for a further 3–5 minutes. Then add the onion and fry for a further 2–3 minutes.
3. Stir in the tomatoes and the remaining dry ingredients. Mix thoroughly. Then reduce the heat and cook for 2–3 minutes.
4. Add the kidney beans and blend in the reserved liquid. Stir, cover and heat through gently. Serve with plain boiled rice and garnish with the fresh chopped coriander. This would go well with a poultry curry such as Moorqi (page 47).

MATAR CHOONDO NE PHOODINO (MUSHY PEAS AND MINT)

50 g (2 oz) butter
1 tablespoon cumin seeds
1 medium onion, peeled and finely chopped
1 × 500 g (19 oz) can mushy peas
2 tablespoons mint sauce
salt
1 sprig fresh mint leaves, to garnish (optional)

Preparation time: 10 minutes
Cooking time: 15 minutes

1. Heat the butter in a pan and fry the cumin seeds and onion together until the onion is soft and transparent.
2. Stir in the peas, then add the mint sauce and salt. Stir thoroughly, then cover and heat through.
3. Garnish with the mint leaves. Serve as part of a main meal with a poultry curry, such as Pot roast chicken (page 48) and Okra and potatoes (page 64).

FROM THE LEFT: Janjado karanga; Janjado

JANJADO (KIDNEY BEAN CURRY)

100 g (4 oz) butter
2 teaspoons cumin seeds
1 large onion, peeled and chopped
1 × 400 g (14 oz) can tomatoes, chopped with the juice
1 tablespoon ground coriander
1 teaspoon chilli powder
1 teaspoon salt
1 teaspoon sugar
2 × 425 g (15 oz) cans kidney beans, drained

Preparation time: 15 minutes
Cooking time: 30–35 minutes

Janjado means kidney beans in Swahili. The beans when fresh are beautifully coloured and naturally freckled. They come in pink, mauve, pinky blue and very dark mauve with dark brown and white speckles. In this country we buy them dried or in cans. The following medium curry is one of many ways in which the beans can be cooked.

1. Heat the butter in a pan, add the cumin seeds and onion together and fry until the onion is light golden brown.
2. Stir in the tomatoes and fry for a few seconds, then add the coriander, chilli, salt and sugar and stir well. Reduce the heat and cook the sauce for about 5–7 minutes.
3. Add the drained beans, stir carefully but thoroughly and heat through for 10–15 minutes.
4. Serve with chapatis to make a satisfying supper dish. For a more substantial meal, accompany with a chicken curry, such as Moorqi (page 47) and plain boiled rice.

Variation:
Dried kidney beans could be used instead of the canned beans. They should first be soaked overnight and then brought to the boil in the same water. Boil for 10 minutes, then reduce the heat and simmer until tender, before using as required.

Most pulses take a long time to cook, so it is a great time-saver to use a pressure cooker. It also saves greatly on the fuel bills. Manufacturers' instructions usually include times for pulses, but as a general rule, cook the pulses for about a third of the time given. Add 1–2 tablespoons oil to the cooking water to prevent the pulses frothing up, which might clog the valve of the pressure cooker.

DOODRI DAAL
(ONIONS AND LENTILS)

600 ml (1 pint) water
225 g (8 oz) dried red lentils
100 g (4 oz) butter
2 large onions, peeled and chopped
2 teaspoons salt
2 teaspoons sugar
1 green chilli, seeded and sliced

Preparation time: 15–20 minutes
Cooking time: 30–45 minutes

1. Place the water and lentils in a saucepan and cook over a gentle heat for about 15–20 minutes or until tender. Reserve.
2. Heat the butter in a pan and fry the onions gently until just soft and transparent.
3. Add the cooked lentils, salt and sugar to the frying pan and stir thoroughly. Reduce the heat, then cover and cook for about 15–20 minutes, stirring occasionally to prevent sticking. Garnish with sliced chilli and serve as a light supper with plain boiled rice and lassi (page 7).

MOONG

225 g (8 oz) moong beans
1.2 litres (2 pints) water
150 g (5 oz) butter
1 tablespoon cumin seeds
1 large onion, peeled and finely chopped
2 cloves garlic, peeled and creamed
2 teaspoons salt
2 teaspoons sugar

Preparation time: 20 minutes
Cooking time: 1¼ hours

1. Place the beans and water in a saucepan. Bring to the boil, then lower the heat. Cover and simmer for 45 minutes or until the beans are tender and have split open.
2. In a separate pan heat the butter and add the cumin seeds and onion. Fry gently until the onion is soft and transparent.
3. Add the creamed garlic and fry for a few seconds then stir in the cooked beans, salt and sugar. Cover and cook for about 25 minutes over a very low heat, adding a little water if necessary. Serve with chapatis and plain boiled rice, Kobi batata (page 69), pickles and chutneys.

MOONG GUJARATI

1.2 litres (2 pints) water
225 g (8 oz) moong beans
2 tablespoons oil
1 teaspoon black mustard seeds
2 teaspoons cumin seeds
good pinch of asafoetida (Hing), (optional)
1 × 400 g (14 oz) can tomatoes, chopped with the juice
1 tablespoon ground coriander
1 green chilli, seeded and halved
2 teaspoons salt
2½ teaspoons sugar
5–6 sprigs fresh coriander leaves, chopped

Preparation time: 10–15 minutes
Cooking time: 1¼ hours

This mild curry makes a good vegetarian meal, served with plain unsweetened yogurt mixed with finely chopped tomatoes or cucumber and rice.

1. Place the water and beans in a saucepan. Bring to the boil, then lower the heat. Cover and simmer for 45 minutes or until the beans are tender and have split open.
2. In a separate pan heat the oil and add the mustard and cumin seeds. Fry until they begin to crackle. Add the asafoetida, if using, and immediately add the cooked beans and stir. (This process should be done with great care as the hot oil will spatter.)
3. Add the remaining ingredients and stir thoroughly. Cover and cook for 25–30 minutes over a low heat, stirring occasionally to prevent sticking.

MASOOR DAAL TAMATAR (LENTIL CURRY)

225 g (8 oz) dried red lentils
450 ml (¾ pint) water
1 quantity Basic curry sauce (page 8)
4 sprigs fresh coriander leaves, chopped, to garnish

Preparation time: 10 minutes
Cooking time: 25–30 minutes

1. Place the water and lentils in a saucepan and cook uncovered, over a gentle heat for about 20–25 minutes or until tender.
2. Stir the curry sauce into the saucepan and cook for a further 5–10 minutes.
3. Garnish with fresh coriander and serve with any dry curry, such as Sukkee kalejee (page 42).

FROM THE LEFT: Moong gujarati; Masoor daal tamatar; Doodri daal

CHANNA BATATA CURRY (CHICK PEAS AND POTATOES)

4 small potatoes, peeled
salt
4 tablespoons oil
1 teaspoon black mustard seeds
1 × 425 g (15 oz) can chick peas, drained
1 tablespoon ground coriander
1 teaspoon turmeric
1 teaspoon chilli powder
5–6 sprigs fresh coriander leaves, chopped

**Preparation time: 30 minutes, plus cooling
Cooking time: 15–20 minutes**

1. Cook the potatoes in boiling salted water until tender. Drain and cool, then cut into cubes.
2. Heat the oil in a separate pan, add the mustard seeds and fry until they begin to pop.
3. Add the remaining ingredients, except the coriander leaves, and the potatoes to the pan. Cook, stirring constantly until heated through and all the spices are thoroughly mixed.
4. Add the chopped coriander and stir for a few seconds, then serve immediately.

KAANDA MATAR (ONION AND PEAS)

50 g (2 oz) butter
1 tablespoon cumin seeds
1 large onion, peeled and chopped
2 cloves garlic, peeled and creamed
1 × 500 g (19 oz) can marrowfat processed peas, drained
5–6 sprigs fresh coriander leaves, chopped

**Preparation time: 25 minutes
Cooking time: 25–30 minutes**

1. Heat the butter in a pan, add the cumin seeds and onion and fry until the onion is soft and transparent.
2. Add the garlic and fry for a few seconds only.
3. Carefully stir in the drained peas. Reduce the heat then cover and heat through, stirring occasionally to prevent sticking.
4. Add the chopped coriander, toss and serve immediately. Accompany with a tomato and onion salad and plain unsweetened yogurt.

Kaanda matar

MATAR DAAL (SPLIT PEAS)

50 ml (2 fl oz) oil
2 teaspoons black mustard seeds
good pinch of asafoetida (Hing), (optional)
225 g (8 oz) split peas, soaked overnight and drained
1 medium onion, peeled and sliced
1 tablespoon ground coriander
2 teaspoons salt
300 ml (½ pint) water
2 sprigs fresh coriander leaves, to garnish

**Preparation time: 15 minutes, plus overnight
    soaking**
Cooking time: 35–45 minutes

1. Heat the oil in a pan and fry the mustard seeds
until they begin to pop. Add the asafoetida, if using,
and immediately stir in the peas.
2. Add the onion, coriander, salt and water. Partially cover the pan and cook over a low heat for 35–
45 minutes, until the peas are tender but still remain
whole. Stir occasionally to prevent sticking.
3. Garnish with the sprigs of coriander and serve
with poppadums and pickles.

PEASE PUDDING TARKA

1 × 425 g (15 oz) can pease pudding
170 ml (7 fl oz) hot water
4 tablespoons oil
4 cloves garlic, peeled and sliced
1 green chilli, trimmed, seeded and halved
salt
To garnish:
2 sprigs fresh coriander leaves
1 lemon, quartered

Preparation time: 10–15 minutes
Cooking time: 15–20 minutes

1. Tip the pease pudding into a bowl and add the
hot water. Mix to a smooth paste and reserve.
2. Heat the oil in a pan, add the garlic and fry until
browned.
3. Carefully stir in the pease pudding mixture, then
add the chilli and salt. Stir continuously to prevent
sticking and heat thoroughly. Add a little more water
if necessary.
4. Serve garnished with coriander sprigs and lemon
quarters.

Matar daal

DAAL BHAJEE
(SPLIT PEAS AND SPINACH)

Serves 6
50 ml (2 fl oz) oil
1 teaspoon cumin seeds
225 g (8 oz) split peas, soaked overnight and drained
1 × 450 g (1 lb) packet frozen spinach, thawed and
    chopped
1 large onion, peeled and sliced
1 tablespoon ground coriander
1 teaspoon chilli powder
1 teaspoon turmeric
salt

**Preparation time: 15–20 minutes, plus soaking
    overnight**
Cooking time: 30–40 minutes

1. Heat the oil in a pan and fry the cumin seeds until
they begin to crackle.
2. Add the remaining ingredients and stir thoroughly. Reduce the heat, then cover and leave the dish to
cook in its own juices, until the peas are tender and
most of the liquid has evaporated.

CHANNA BATATA CURRY
(CHICK PEAS AND POTATOES)

4 small potatoes, peeled
salt
4 tablespoons oil
1 teaspoon mustard seeds
1 × 425 g (15 oz) can chick peas, drained
1 tablespoon ground coriander
1 teaspoon chilli powder
1 × 225 g (8 oz) can tomatoes, chopped with the juice
1 tablespoon tomato purée
1 tablespoon brown sugar
sprigs of fresh coriander leaves, to garnish

Preparation time: 30 minutes, plus cooling
Cooking time: 15–20 minutes

1. Cook the potatoes in boiling salted water until
tender. Drain and cool, then cut into cubes.
2. Heat the oil in a separate pan, add the mustard
seeds and fry until they begin to pop. Add the peas
and potatoes and toss them in the oil and seeds. Stir
in the coriander and chilli powder.
3. Stir in the tomatoes, tomato purée, sugar and salt,
then cover and heat through. Serve garnished with
the coriander, accompanied by plain boiled rice.

FROM THE FRONT: Channa batata curry; Daal bhajee

VEGETABLES

BAINGAN BATATA (AUBERGINE AND POTATOES)

50 ml (2 fl oz) oil
1 teaspoon fenugreek seeds
1 teaspoon black mustard seeds
3 medium potatoes, about 450 g (1 lb), peeled and cubed
1 medium aubergine, about 175–225 g (6–8 oz), cubed
1 tablespoon ground coriander
1 teaspoon chilli powder
1 teaspoon turmeric
1 teaspoon sugar
1–2 teaspoons salt
1 × 225 g (8 oz) can tomatoes, chopped with the juice
50 ml (2 fl oz) water
5–6 sprigs fresh coriander leaves, chopped, to garnish

Preparation time: 10–15 minutes
Cooking time: 30–40 minutes

1. Heat the oil in a large pan, add the fenugreek seeds and fry until browned. Then add the mustard seeds and fry until they begin to pop.
2. Carefully add the potatoes and aubergine, reduce the heat, cover the pan and fry for a few seconds.
3. Add the spices, sugar and salt, and stir well.
4. Add the tomatoes and water and mix thoroughly. Cover and cook over a low heat for about 30 minutes, stirring occasionally during the cooking time.
5. Serve garnished with chopped coriander. If serving as a lunchtime dish, accompany with plain boiled rice and Pease pudding tarka (page 61) or Moong (page 58). For a more substantial meal, serve with a fish or meat curry as well.

SOOKKA BHINDA (CURRIED OKRA)

450 g (1 lb) okra
50 ml (2 fl oz) oil
1 teaspoon fenugreek seeds
1 tablespoon ground coriander
1 teaspoon turmeric
1 teaspoon chilli powder
salt
5–6 sprigs fresh coriander leaves, chopped, to garnish

Preparation time: 25 minutes
Cooking time: 30–35 minutes

BHINDA BATATA (OKRA AND POTATOES)

450 g (1 lb) okra
225 g (8 oz) potatoes
4 tablespoons oil
1 teaspoon black mustard seeds
1 medium onion, peeled and sliced lengthways
1 teaspoon salt
1 teaspoon turmeric
1 teaspoon chilli powder
1 tablespoon ground coriander
2 tomatoes, chopped
4 sprigs fresh coriander leaves, chopped, to garnish

Preparation time: 25 minutes
Cooking time: 30–40 minutes

1. Wipe the okra with a damp cloth, top and tail them and cut each one in half. Cut each half into 4 lengthways and reserve.
2. Peel and wash the potatoes, cut them into 2.5 cm (1 inch) cubes and reserve.
3. In a pan, heat the oil and fry the mustard seeds until they begin to pop. Then add the onion and fry quickly for 2–3 minutes.
4. Reduce the heat and carefully add the prepared vegetables. Add the salt, turmeric, chilli and ground coriander and toss the ingredients well.
5. Cover and cook for about 25 minutes, tossing the vegetables every few minutes.
6. Stir in the chopped tomatoes, toss well and open cook for a further 10–15 minutes. Serve sprinkled with chopped fresh coriander.

1. Wipe the okra with a damp cloth. Trim and cut into 2.5 cm (1 inch) rings.
2. Heat the oil in a pan and fry the fenugreek seeds until browned.
3. Add the prepared okra, ground coriander, turmeric, chilli and salt and toss to mix well.
4. Cook uncovered over a low heat, tossing frequently until the okra is tender and dry. Serve sprinkled with fresh coriander.

FROM THE BOTTOM: Bhinda batata; Sookha bhinda

BAINGAN RAVAIYA (STUFFED AUBERGINE)

100 g (4 oz) fresh unroasted peanuts, finely ground
25 g (1 oz) sesame seeds
150 ml (¼ pint) oil
2 tablespoons ground coriander
1 tablespoon garam masala powder
1 teaspoon turmeric
2 teaspoons salt
2 teaspoons sugar
2 medium tomatoes, chopped
4–6 small aubergines, about 100–175 g (4–6 oz) each

Preparation time: 30 minutes
Cooking time: 30–40 minutes
Oven: 180°C, 325°F, Gas Mark 4

For this medium curry, use the small, round aubergines available in most Asian shops or alternatively look for the smallest ones you can find. These retain their shape during cooking, so as to look more attractive when served. Leave the stalks on and make sure the stuffing is firm in order to help the aubergines remain whole.

1. In a bowl, mix together the peanuts, sesame seeds, 50 ml (2 fl oz) of the oil, spices, salt, sugar and chopped tomatoes.
2. Wash and wipe the aubergines and leave the stalks on. Make a deep cut lengthways on one side to form a pocket in each aubergine, making sure not to cut through.
3. Stuff each aubergine with some filling, pressing the mixture carefully but firmly into each aubergine. Brush the aubergines with oil and reserve.
4. Spread the remaining oil in a baking dish and smooth any leftover stuffing over it.
5. Place the aubergines in the baking dish and cover with foil. Cook in a preheated oven for 30 minutes. Remove the foil and continue cooking for a further 10 minutes. Serve with chapatis or plain boiled rice, chutneys and plain unsweetened yogurt mixed with finely diced cucumber and sprinkled with paprika.

BAKED CAULIFLOWER

1 medium cauliflower, about 750 g (1½ lb), trimmed, leaving some tender stalks around
1 quantity Basic curry sauce (page 8)
50 g (2 oz) desiccated coconut

Preparation time: 20 minutes
Cooking time: 25–30 minutes
Oven: 200°C, 400°F, Gas Mark 6

A whole cauliflower requires skill to cook satisfactorily. Very often the centre remains uncooked and the sides fall apart as they get overcooked. To ensure even cooking, the cauliflower is best parboiled before baking.

1. Make a deep cross cut about 7.5 cm (3 inches) long in the centre of the cauliflower core. Parboil in boiling salted water for 7–10 minutes only. Lift out and drain thoroughly. Transfer to a deep ovenproof dish.
2. Combine the curry sauce and coconut then pour over the cauliflower. Cover and cook in a preheated oven for about 20 minutes until tender.
3. Carefully place the cauliflower on a warm serving dish and spoon over the remaining sauce.

BHARELA BHINDA (STUFFED OKRA)

450 g (1 lb) large okra
85 ml (3 fl oz) oil
1 medium onion, peeled and minced
1 tablespoon ground coriander
1 tablespoon garam masala powder
1 teaspoon chilli powder
1 teaspoon turmeric
1 teaspoon salt
1 tablespoon tomato purée

Preparation time: 30 minutes
Cooking time: 25–30 minutes

When preparing okra, it is important to remember that they should never be washed under running water before cooking, as this makes them slimy. Simply wipe them with a damp cloth or with moistened paper towels. Discard any that are damaged.

KOBI GAAJER (CABBAGE AND CARROTS)

Serves 6
85 ml (3 fl oz) oil
1 tablespoon cumin seeds
450 g (1 lb) white cabbage, finely shredded
225 g (8 oz) carrots, peeled and diced
1 tablespoon ground coriander
1 teaspoon chilli powder
2 teaspoons salt
1 × 225 g (8 oz) can tomatoes, chopped with the juice
5–6 sprigs fresh coriander leaves, chopped, to garnish

Preparation time: 20–25 minutes
Cooking time: 35–45 minutes

1. Heat the oil in a large pan and fry the cumin seeds until they crackle.
2. Carefully add the cabbage and carrots. Reduce the heat and add the ground coriander, chilli powder and salt and mix well.
3. Stir in the tomatoes. Cover and cook over a low heat for about 30–45 minutes, stirring frequently, until almost dry.
4. Sprinkle with fresh coriander and serve with saffron rice. This dry curry would go well with one of the meat curries such as Lamb curry in the oven (page 31).

A dry curry originating from Gujarat in India. The stuffing varies from district to district. It is essential to use young, unblemished okra as they are cooked untrimmed.

1. Wipe the okra with a damp cloth. Make a slit on one side of each okra to form a pocket and reserve.
2. In a bowl, combine 2 tablespoons oil with the remaining ingredients, and mix well. Use the mixture to stuff each okra, pressing it well into the pocket.
3. Heat the remaining oil in a pan and gently lower the stuffed okra into the oil. Cook uncovered over a medium heat for about 25 minutes, tossing frequently to prevent sticking.
4. To serve, arrange attractively on a warm serving dish. Serve with sliced banana.

CLOCKWISE FROM THE FRONT: Baked cauliflower; Bharela bhinda; Kobi gaajer

KOBI BATATA
(CABBAGE AND POTATOES)

450 g (1 lb) potatoes, washed
50 ml (2 fl oz) oil
1 teaspoon cumin seeds
450 g (1 lb) white cabbage, shredded
1 tablespoon ground coriander
1 green chilli, seeded and finely chopped
1 teaspoon turmeric
salt
6 medium tomatoes, chopped
5–6 sprigs fresh coriander leaves, chopped

Preparation time: 30 minutes
Cooking time: 30–40 minutes

This curry was very popular among the Kutchi people in Kampala. It is still popular among the Kutchi people in this country. Kutchis are strict vegetarians and eat simple food with little or no spices, reflecting their traditional style of living.

1. Cut the potatoes in half lengthways, then cut each half into 4, lengthways.
2. Heat the oil in a large pan, add the cumin seeds and fry them until they crackle.

3. Carefully add the potatoes, cabbage, the spices and salt. Stir well, then cover and cook over a low heat until the potatoes are tender. Stir or toss frequently to prevent sticking.
4. Add the chopped tomatoes and chopped coriander. Stir well and cook, partly covered, for a further 7–10 minutes. Serve as part of a meal together with Moong gujarati (page 59) and plain boiled rice.

Trim tops off chillis.

Slice lengthways and remove seeds.

Chop up finely.

MAKAI DANAA (SWEETCORN CURRY)

50 ml (2 fl oz) oil
1 tablespoon cumin seeds
1 × 450 g (1 lb) packet frozen sweetcorn kernels
1 teaspoon ground coriander
1 teaspoon garam masala powder
5–6 sprigs fresh coriander leaves, chopped
salt
4 tomatoes, chopped
1 tomato, sliced, to garnish

Preparation time: 5–10 minutes
Cooking time: 20–25 minutes

Kaasori is the Swahili name for sweetcorn in Uganda. However, in Kenya it is known as Mahindi meaning Indian. The Indian traders made it popular in the very early 1900s as they came down to settle in the East African coast.

1. Heat the oil in a pan, and fry the cumin seeds until they crackle.
2. Add the sweetcorn, ground coriander, garam masala, chopped fresh coriander, salt and tomatoes and stir well. Cover and cook over a gentle heat for about 20–25 minutes.
3. Serve garnished with slices of tomato.

Variation:
2 × 425 g (14½ oz) cans sweetcorn kernels, drained, may be used in place of the frozen sweetcorn. After step 1, all ingredients can be stir-fried together until heated through.

CAULIFLOWER RANGEEN (CAULIFLOWER IN COLOURS)

50 ml (2 fl oz) oil
1 tablespoon cumin seeds
1 medium onion, peeled and sliced
450 g (1 lb) cauliflower, divided into florets
100 g (4 oz) fresh or frozen peas
100 g (4 oz) carrots, peeled and cut into strips about 5 cm (2 inches) long
1 tablespoon ground coriander
1 teaspoon turmeric
1 teaspoon chilli powder
salt
5–6 sprigs fresh coriander leaves, chopped

Preparation time: 30 minutes
Cooking time: 35–45 minutes

1. Heat the oil in a large pan, and fry the cumin seeds until they crackle.
2. Add the onion and fry quickly until lightly browned.
3. Reduce the heat and carefully add the prepared vegetables and the remaining ingredients (except the fresh coriander).
4. Stir well, cover and cook the vegetables in their own juices over a low heat until they are tender and most of the liquid has evaporated.
5. A few minutes before serving, sprinkle the chopped coriander over the vegetables. Cook uncovered for a further 5 minutes, tossing frequently. Serve immediately with chapatis, plain boiled rice, plain unsweetened yogurt and lassi (page 7) sprinkled with grated lime.

KHAT MALAI PHOOLKOBI (CAULIFLOWER AND PEPPER IN SOUR CREAM)

50 ml (2 fl oz) oil
1 tablespoon cumin seeds
450 g (1 lb) cauliflower, divided into florets
1 large green pepper, cored, seeded and sliced lengthways
1 teaspoon turmeric
1–2 green chillis, seeded and finely chopped
1 teaspoon garlic powder
salt
300 ml (½ pint) soured cream

Preparation time: 20 minutes
Cooking time: 30–40 minutes

1. Heat the oil in a large pan, and fry the cumin seeds until they crackle.
2. Reduce the heat and carefully add the cauliflower. Reserve 4 strips of pepper for garnish and add the rest to the pan. Add the remaining dry ingredients and mix thoroughly.
3. Partly cover the pan and cook until the vegetables are tender and dry. Toss the mixture frequently during the cooking time.
4. Whisk the soured cream and stir into the vegetable mixture and heat through without boiling.
5. Serve garnished with the reserved strips of pepper. This medium curry makes a good accompaniment to Tandoori pork chops (page 39).

CLOCKWISE FROM THE FRONT: Fried courgettes; Cauliflower rangeen; Makai danaa

FRIED COURGETTES

50 g (2 oz) butter
1 medium onion, peeled and finely chopped
6–8 medium courgettes, trimmed and cut into 1 cm
    (½ inch) slices
1 tablespoon cumin seeds, finely ground
½ teaspoon ground nutmeg
1 teaspoon chilli powder
1 teaspoon turmeric
salt

Preparation time: 15–20 minutes
Cooking time: 15–20 minutes

A dry curry which is quick and easy to prepare. Choose courgettes which are 10–15 cm (4–6 inches) long.

1. Heat the butter in a frying pan, add the onion and courgettes and stir-fry for 10 minutes.
2. Add the remaining ingredients and stir-fry for a further 5–10 minutes.
3. Serve either as a starter on their own or with a dry fish dish, such as Copra matchi (page 11).

SHAAK MISHRAAN (MIXED VEGETABLES)

2–3 tablespoons oil
1 medium carrot, peeled and diced
1 medium onion, peeled and diced
1 medium potato, peeled and diced
1 small cauliflower, divided into florets
1 tablespoon ground coriander
1 tablespoon garam masala powder
1 teaspoon chilli powder
salt
5–6 sprigs fresh coriander leaves, coarsely chopped

Preparation time: 25 minutes
Cooking time: 25–30 minutes

This is a spicy dry curry which keeps for up to 5 days in the refrigerator.

1. Place the oil in a large pan over a low heat. Add all the ingredients and stir well.
2. Cover and cook until the vegetables are tender. Stir occasionally, making sure that each time the lid is lifted no water falls back into the vegetables. This ensures the dryness of the curry.

FATHER'S SAFARI POTATOES

6 medium potatoes, washed
salt
50 ml (2 fl oz) oil
1 teaspoon cumin seeds
pinch of asafoetida (Hing), (optional)
1 teaspoon turmeric
1 green chilli, seeded and finely chopped
3–4 sprigs fresh coriander leaves, chopped

Preparation time: 30 minutes, plus cooling
Cooking time: 5–10 minutes

1. Cook the potatoes in boiling salted water until tender. Drain and cool. When cold, skin the potatoes and cut into 2.5 cm (1 inch) cubes.
2. Heat the oil in a pan, add the cumin seeds and fry them until they crackle. Reduce the heat.
3. Add the asafoetida, if using, and carefully add the potatoes.
4. Add the remaining ingredients and cook for 5–10 minutes to heat through. Toss frequently to mix the spices well.
5. Serve with chapatis.

FROM THE BOTTOM: Curly kale bhajee batata; Shaak mishraan

LEEK BATALA (LEEK AND POTATOES)

50 ml (2 fl oz) oil
1 teaspoon black mustard seeds
225 g (8 oz) potatoes, washed and cubed
450 g (1 lb) leeks, trimmed, washed and cut into 2.5 cm (1 inch) lengths
1 tablespoon cumin seeds, crushed
1 teaspoon ground cinnamon
1 teaspoon turmeric
1 teaspoon chilli powder
salt
50 ml (2 fl oz) water

Preparation time: 25 minutes
Cooking time: 30–35 minutes
Oven: 180°C, 350°F, Gas Mark 4

This is a dry curry, which is fried first on top of the stove, and then baked, covered in the oven, until cooked. The idea is to retain the shape of the beautiful rings of leek.

1. Heat the oil in a pan, add the mustard seeds and fry them until they pop.
2. Carefully add the prepared vegetables and the remaining ingredients and stir to mix well.
3. Transfer to an ovenproof casserole, cover and cook in a preheated oven for 30–35 minutes or until the vegetables are tender. Serve as an accompaniment to Daal chicken (page 46) with Moong gujarati (page 59) and plain boiled rice.

CURLY KALE BHAJEE BATATA (KALE AND POTATOES)

50 ml (2 fl oz) oil
450 g (1 lb) kale, washed and shredded
225 g (8 oz) potatoes, peeled and cut into 2.5 cm (1 inch) cubes
1 medium onion, peeled and sliced
1 tablespoon ground coriander
1 teaspoon turmeric
salt

Preparation time: 30 minutes
Cooking time: 25–30 minutes

1. Place the oil and the remaining ingredients in a large pan and stir-fry over a low heat for a few minutes to mix well.
2. Cover and leave the vegetables to cook in their own juices, until the potatoes are tender and most of the liquid has evaporated, about 25 minutes.

KAANDA BATATA (ONION AND POTATOES)

50 ml (2 fl oz) oil
1 teaspoon black mustard seeds
750 g (1½ lb) potatoes, peeled and cubed
1 large onion, peeled and sliced
1 teaspoon ground coriander
1 teaspoon chilli powder
1 teaspoon turmeric
salt
600 ml (1 pint) water

Preparation time: 25 minutes
Cooking time: 25–30 minutes

This recipe is a warming, mildly flavoured, saucy curry.

1. Heat the oil in a pan, add the mustard seeds and fry them until they pop.
2. Reduce the heat and carefully add the remaining ingredients (except the water) and toss to mix well.
3. Add the water gradually, stirring carefully, increase the heat slightly, then cover and cook until the potatoes are just tender.
4. Before serving lift out a few pieces of potato and mash them. Return the mashed potatoes to the pan and stir thoroughly to thicken the sauce.
5. Serve with a dry meat or vegetable curry such as Bholar gosht (page 20) or Stuffed okra (page 68).

MATAR DAAL MARROW (MARROW AND SPLIT PEAS)

50 ml (2 fl oz) oil
1 teaspoon black mustard seeds
pinch of asafoetida (Hing), (optional)
1 medium onion, peeled and sliced
225 g (8 oz) split peas, soaked overnight and drained
300 ml (½ pint) water
1 tablespoon ground coriander
1 teaspoon chilli powder
1 teaspoon turmeric
salt
450 g (1 lb) marrow, peeled and cut into 2.5 cm (1 inch) cubes

Preparation time: 15 minutes, plus soaking overnight
Cooking time: 30–40 minutes

1. Heat the oil in a large pan, add the mustard seeds and fry them until they pop. Reduce the heat, carefully add the asafoetida, if using, and immediately add the drained peas and onion. Cover the pan for a few seconds to preserve the flavour.
2. Add the water, ground coriander, chilli, turmeric and salt and stir well. Bring to the boil. Reduce the heat and cook partially covered for about 20 minutes.
3. Add the prepared marrow, stir, cover and cook until completely tender.

BAINGAN MATAR
(AUBERGINE AND PEAS)

50 ml (2 fl oz) oil
1 teaspoon fenugreek seeds
1 teaspoon black mustard seeds
1 teaspoon cumin seeds
450 g (1 lb) fresh or frozen peas
1 medium aubergine, about 175 g–225 g (6–8 oz), trimmed
   and cut into cubes
1 tablespoon ground coriander
1 teaspoon chilli powder
1 teaspoon turmeric
salt
1 × 225 g (8 oz) can tomatoes, chopped with the juice
50 ml (2 fl oz) water
5–6 sprigs fresh coriander leaves, chopped

Preparation time: 10–15 minutes
Cooking time: 30–40 minutes

1. Heat the oil in a pan, add the fenugreek seeds and fry until browned. Then add the mustard and cumin seeds and fry until they begin to pop.
2. Carefully add the peas and aubergine, reduce the heat, cover the pan and fry for a few seconds only.
3. Add the spices and salt, and stir well.
4. Add the tomatoes and water and mix thoroughly. Cover and cook for about 30 minutes, stirring once or twice during the cooking time.
5. A few minutes before serving, add the chopped coriander, stir and complete the cooking time. Serve with a meat or chicken curry of your choice.

BHAJEE BAINGAN
(SPINACH AND AUBERGINE)

1 large aubergine
50 ml (2 fl oz) oil
1 teaspoon fenugreek seeds
1 × 450 g (1 lb) packet frozen spinach, thawed and
   chopped
1 medium onion, peeled and sliced
1 tablespoon ground coriander
1 teaspoon turmeric
salt

Preparation time: 10 minutes
Cooking time: 30–35 minutes

This mild spiced curry makes a good accompaniment to a meal with spicy meat curries, such as Pork and haricot beans (page 36). It can also be eaten with chapatis and plain unsweetened yogurt as a light lunch.

1. Wash and trim the aubergine, then cut into strips, 5 × 2.5 cm (2 × 1 inch). Reserve in a bowl of cold water to prevent discolouring. Before using drain and dry on paper towels.
2. Heat the oil in a pan, add the fenugreek seeds and fry them until browned.
3. Reduce the heat and carefully add the aubergine, spinach, onion, coriander, turmeric and salt. Stir well, then cover and cook the vegetables in their own juices until tender.

Variation:
Fresh spinach can be used in place of frozen spinach, in which case it may be necessary to add a little water. Add the salt sparingly at first as the bulk of raw chopped spinach cooks down to a small mass. Taste and adjust seasoning when cooked.

Cut off stalk.

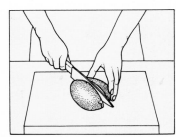
Slice aubergine lengthways.

Cut up into cubes.

FROM THE LEFT: kaanda batata; Bhajee baingan; Baingan matar

MATAR BATATA 1 (PEAS AND POTATOES)

50 g (2 oz) butter
225 g (8 oz) fresh or frozen peas
225 g (8 oz) potatoes, peeled and diced
225 g (8 oz) onions, peeled and diced
1 tablespoon garam masala powder
1 teaspoon turmeric
1 teaspoon chilli powder

Preparation time: 30 minutes
Cooking time: 25–30 minutes

1. Heat the butter in a pan, add all the ingredients and stir-fry for a few minutes to mix well.
2. Cover and cook over a low heat for about 25–30 minutes or until the vegetables are tender. Stir occasionally during the cooking time to prevent sticking.
3. Serve as an accompaniment to meat.

MATAR BATATA 2 (GUJARATI)

50 ml (2 fl oz) oil
½ teaspoon fenugreek seeds
1 teaspoon black mustard seeds
pinch of asafoetida (Hing), (optional)
4 medium potatoes, peeled and cut into 2.5 cm (1 inch) cubes
225 g (8 oz) fresh or frozen peas
1 tablespoon ground coriander
1 teaspoon turmeric
1 teaspoon chilli powder
1 × 225 g (8 oz) can tomatoes, chopped with the juice
salt
1 teaspoon sugar

Preparation time: 10 minutes
Cooking time: 30–35 minutes

Peas and potatoes cooked in this Gujarati way taste quite different from the previous recipe. They are moist and slightly tangy in taste.

1. Heat the oil in a pan, add the fenugreek seeds and fry them until browned. Add the mustard seeds and fry them until they pop. Reduce the heat, add asafoetida, if using, immediately add the vegetables and cover to preserve the flavour.
2. Uncover and add the remaining ingredients (except the fresh coriander). Cover and cook, stirring occasionally, until the vegetables are tender and most of the liquid has reduced to a thickened sauce.

FUNCY BATATA
(FRENCH BEANS AND POTATOES)

50 g (2 oz) butter
1 medium onion, peeled and sliced
4 medium potatoes, peeled and cut into 2.5 cm (1 inch)
    cubes
450 g (1 lb) green beans, sliced (fresh or frozen)
1 teaspoon ground mixed spice
1 teaspoon ground cinnamon
1 teaspoon turmeric
1 teaspoon cumin seeds, crushed
salt

Preparation time: 20–25 minutes
Cooking time: 30–35 minutes

1. Heat the butter in a large pan and add all the
ingredients. Toss to mix well.
2. Cover and cook over a low heat until the vegetables are tender. If using fresh beans, it may be
necessary to add 2–3 tablespoons water.

FUNCY SHAAK
(RUNNER BEAN CURRY)

50 ml (2 fl oz) oil
1 teaspoon black mustard seeds
750 g (1½ lb) runner beans, trimmed and sliced on the
    slant into 2 cm (¾ inch) thick slices
1 medium onion, peeled and sliced
1 tablespoon ground coriander
1 teaspoon garam masala powder
1 teaspoon chilli powder
1 × 225 g (8 oz) can tomatoes, chopped with the juice
salt

Preparation time: 25 minutes
Cooking time: 25–30 minutes

1. Heat the oil in a pan, add the mustard seeds and
fry them until they pop.
2. Reduce the heat and carefully add the prepared
beans and onion.
3. Add the ground coriander, garam masala and
chilli powder and mix well.
4. Add the remaining ingredients and stir well.
Cover and cook over a low heat until tender. Stir
occasionally during the cooking time to prevent
sticking.

CLOCKWISE FROM THE FRONT: Funcy shaak; Matar batata 1; Funcy batata

MUGFALIWALA RINGAN BATATA (POTATOES AND AUBERGINE IN PEANUTS)

120 ml (4 fl oz) oil
2 teaspoons cumin seeds
100 g (4 oz) fresh, unroasted peanuts, ground
1 medium onion, peeled and chopped
6 medium potatoes, peeled and cut into 2.5 cm (1 inch) cubes
1 large aubergine, cut into 2.5 cm (1 inch) cubes
1 × 400 g (14 oz) can tomatoes, chopped with the juice
300 ml (½ pint) water
1 tablespoon ground coriander
1 teaspoon garam masala powder
1 teaspoon chilli powder
1 teaspoon turmeric
2 teaspoons salt

Preparation time: 30–35 minutes
Cooking time: 30–40 minutes

1. Heat the oil in a large pan, add the cumin seeds and fry them until they pop.
2. Add the ground peanuts and fry for 1 minute only.
3. Reduce the heat, add the onion and fry for a further minute.
4. Add the prepared vegetables and stir-fry for a few seconds. Then add the remaining ingredients. Stir well, then cover and cook over a low heat, for about 25–30 minutes. Stir occasionally during the cooking time to prevent sticking.
5. Serve with chapatis or naan.

BHAJEE KAANDA (SPINACH AND ONION)

50 ml (2 fl oz) oil
1 teaspoon fenugreek seeds
1 × 450 g (1 lb) packet frozen spinach, thawed and chopped
225 g (8 oz) onions, peeled and sliced
1 tablespoon ground coriander
1 teaspoon garam masala powder
1 teaspoon chilli powder
1 teaspoon turmeric
salt

Preparation time: 10–15 minutes
Cooking time: 20–25 minutes

KHUTTA MITHA BATATA (SWEET AND SOUR POTATO CURRY)

50 ml (2 fl oz) oil
1 teaspoon black mustard seeds
1 teaspoon cumin seeds
6 medium potatoes, peeled and cubed
2 teaspoons ground coriander
1 teaspoon turmeric
1 teaspoon chilli powder
2 teaspoons salt
4 teaspoons brown sugar
300 ml (½ pint) water
1 × 75 g (3 oz) can tomato purée
3 tablespoons vinegar
5–6 sprigs fresh coriander leaves, chopped, to garnish

Preparation time: 10–15 minutes
Cooking time: 25–30 minutes

1. Heat the oil in a pan, add the mustard and cumin seeds together and fry them until they pop.
2. Reduce the heat and carefully add the potatoes.
3. Add the remaining ingredients and stir well. Cover and cook over a low heat until the potatoes are tender, and a large amount of thick sauce remains in the pan.
4. Serve garnished with the chopped fresh coriander.

This medium vegetable curry makes a delicious accompanying dish with any meal in summer, when fresh spinach is plentiful. If using frozen spinach, it will be easier to chop when only partially thawed, but allow to thaw completely before using.

1. Heat the oil in a pan, add the fenugreek seeds and fry until browned.
2. Reduce the heat, then carefully add the spinach and the remaining ingredients. Mix thoroughly.
3. Cover and leave the vegetables to cook in their own juices for about 20–25 minutes.
4. For a complete meal, serve with Masoor daal tamatar (page 59), Kuku paka (page 48), chapatis and rice. Pickles and chutneys will add extra interest.

FROM THE BOTTOM: Bhajee kaanda; Mugfaliwala ringan batata; Khutta mitha batata

INDEX